RELIGION AND VIOLENCE

Books by ROBERT McAFEE BROWN
Published by THE WESTMINSTER PRESS

Religion and Violence

The Pseudonyms of God

The Collect'd Writings of St. Hereticus

The Significance of the Church
(Layman's Theological Library)

The Bible Speaks to You

P. T. Forsyth: Prophet for Today

RELIGION AND VIOLENCE

A Primer for White Americans

by
Robert McAfee Brown

THE WESTMINSTER PRESS
PHILADELPHIA

PUBLISHED BY THE WESTMINSTER PRESS ®
PHILADELPHIA, PENNSYLVANIA

PRINTED IN THE UNITED STATES OF AMERICA

Library of Congress Cataloging in Publication Data

Brown, Robert McAfee, 1920–
   Religion and violence.

   Bibliography: p.
   1. Violence—Moral and religious aspects.
I. Title.
BT736.15.B76   261.8′73   73–14710
ISBN 0–664–24977–9

TABLE OF CONTENTS

Credits

The illustrations throughout this book are from the work of Kaethe Kollwitz. This German-born artist is a favorite of Professor Brown's, and several volumes of her prints and drawings are in the Brown family library.

COVER *Mothers.* Lithograph, 1919. Klipstein catalog number 135. Permission to reproduce this and the other works listed according to the Klipstein catalog number has been granted by Kornfeld and Klipstein of Bern, Switzerland.

PAGE XVI *Parents.* Lithograph, 1920. Klipstein no. 144.

PAGE 14 *Killed in Action!* Lithograph, 1921. Klipstein no. 153.

PAGE 28 *Death Reaching Out After Children,* from Series *"Death,"* sheet 4. Lithograph, 1934-35. Klipstein no. 259.

PAGE 40 *Germany's Children are Starving.* Lithograph, 1923. Klipstein no. 190.

PAGE 54 *Death Consoling,* from Series *"Parting and Death."* Black chalk, about 1923. Courtesy Kunstmuseum Bern.

PAGE 72 *Woman, Fondling Child.* Charcoal drawing, about 1920. Städtische Kunsthalle Mannheim.

PAGE 90 *Uniting in Brotherhood (Verbrüderung).* Lithograph, 1924. Klipstein no. 199.

A SHORT PREFACE WITH A LONG FOOTNOTE

Be realistic. Ask for the impossible.
> graffito in Paris during the 1968
> student uprisings of Nanterre

The following pages embody a slight modification of the Parisian students' demands. The task I have set myself is to respond to the imperative, "Be realistic. *Attempt* the impossible." This translates into: "Write a small book on religion and violence." I do not think it would be difficult to write a large book on such a subject; indeed, there are many of them, a lot of which I have read. But the issue is so pressing, and our time for reflection on pressing issues is so fleeting, that it seemed to me important to keep the discussion brief, and to distill the wisdom of many pages by others into the modest compass of my own. Readers who desire more ample fare are directed to the bibliography, where they will find it in abundance.

Among many liabilities, there is at least one asset to writing a short book: the author can arbitrarily exclude certain topics from consideration on the ground that inclusion would unduly lengthen his presentation and thereby defeat his purpose. I have limited the discussion largely to American instances of violence, not because other races or nations are guiltless, but because I believe it is salutary first of all to set one's own house in order. I have excluded the whole area of the psychological approach to violence (are we violence-prone and aggressive by nature?) as beyond space limitations and my own competence. I have not, except briefly, reworked the whole "pacifist-nonpacifist" controversy, nor have I given detailed attention to Jesus' teaching on such matters. I have not tried to provide a "how-to" manual on violent or nonviolent techniques.

And I have not even put forth a tidy, crystal-clear set of conclusions on the subject of the book.

The last point deserves brief amplification. My own odyssey on the matter of religion and violence has been variegated if not circuitous. I would like to have arrived at a position that I could unambiguously commend to others as appropriate in all instances. My quest has not been blessed with that kind of certainty, but I believe I have uncovered some realities that may be useful to others on similar quests of their own. Consequently, the purpose of this book is not to announce to others where they ought to be on the issue of religion and violence; it is to give them materials with which they can figure out for themselves where they ought to be.

As the subtitle indicates, I address myself in the first instance to "white Americans." I hope others will read the book, at least to find out how one white American thinks about problems that affect the whole human family, but I am not confident that a white American has much moral leverage for telling a black American, or a brown Latin American, or an African of any hue, just how he should act in his own particular situation. I have to take very seriously the acid words of Jean Genet in commenting on the usual advice of whites to blacks:

> It is evident that recommending nonviolence to blacks is an effort to retain the Christian vocabulary which has kept them imprisoned in passivity for so long. However Christian the whites are, they don't feel guilty about using guns: that is violence. Asking blacks in America to be nonviolent means that whites are demanding a Christian virtue which they themselves do not possess. That means that whites are once again trying to dupe the blacks (*Ramparts*, June 1970, p. 31).

While it may be important to be circumspect about offering ethical advice to nonwhites, I believe I am entitled to press some matters onto the consciences of white Americans. This is particularly important because an extraordinary proportion of the violence unleashed in the world today is the responsibility and fault of white Americans. There are few audiences, in other words, to whom a discussion of religion and violence could be more appropriately and more importunately addressed. If such readers feel that too much blame is being laid on them, I remind them that I am one of their number and that I, too, squirm. The Biblical insight that **"to whomsoever much is given of him shall much be required"** (Luke 12:48) is not inconsequential moralizing but a descriptive law of life; white Americans who have been given so much can expect a high degree of accountability to be laid at their door, not only by less fortunate human beings, but by God as well.

The specific aims of this book are to sensitize us to the real and *hidden* violence in our society, and to push beyond conventional understandings of the word that let us off the hook and enable us to lapse back into complacency. We will focus on ourselves in the uncomfortable light by which we are seen by others, specifically those in the "third world"—a term that subsequent discussion will seek to clarify, and which for the moment can stand for the vast majority of the human family that is nonrich and nonwhite. Today every problem, including violence, is a global problem, and we must never be allowed to forget it.

I have had the advantage of presenting this material to a number of diverse groups and profiting from their responses. An abbreviated version was first discussed at a ministers' conference at Union Theological Seminary in the summer of 1969. It was expanded for the Stanford Summer Alumni College of 1971 and formed the substance of the Homer J. Armstrong Lectures at Kalamazoo College in November 1971. Recast, it was presented to ministerial groups at the Princeton Summer Institute of Theology in July 1972 and to a conference of Methodist ministers in Michigan in August of the same year. In something close to its present form, it was presented as the Jaymes Morgan Memorial Lectures at Fuller Theological Seminary in January 1973, at Alaska Methodist University in March, and at the ecumenically sponsored Portland Christian Lectureship in April. On each of these occasions the ideas were given spirited critique from which I benefited immensely.

Monica Moore and Minako Sano, who typed the manuscript, gave editorial suggestions that increased clarity, while Sheila Cahill of the Stanford Alumni Association and Paul Meacham of Westminster Press provided help throughout. Craig Schindler, a law student, and David Gill, of the World Council of Churches, made substantive suggestions during the process of editing.

My greatest indebtedness, however, is to a decade of my own students at Stanford University, especially the members of two freshman seminars on religion and violence. On this particular topic they have all been my constant teachers and have forced me, by the strength and costliness of their own commitments, to open up issues that a certain middle-aged timidity on my part might otherwise have been content to leave unexplored.

Robert McAfee Brown

Stanford University
April 1973

An Autobiographical Footnote

While I do not want to lend my own spiritual pilgrimage the dignity of ten-point type, I believe some readers may find it useful to know how I have personally come to such conclusions as I have reached. Violence is not an academic issue, any more than religion is an academic issue, and although much of what follows will attempt to report carefully and fairly the viewpoints of others, it is impossible to discuss a subject as volatile as this one without one's own presuppositions and prejudices entering into the reporting. It may therefore be useful for readers to know something of the background out of which I approach the material so that they may assess the cogency that the argument has for them. Those who find such considerations inconsequential can proceed directly to the first chapter.

As a member of a "liberal" Protestant church in the 1930s, I was brought up with the notion that pacifism was the only legitimate Christian position. We knew how baleful had been the impact of World War I on our society, and it was a commonplace that those who had sown a Versailles Treaty could only reap the whirlwind of a Hitler. We believed with the Kellogg-Briand Pact that war must be forever renounced as an instrument of international policy, and that the only possible Christian position was a total renunciation of war, force, and all means of violence.

It is much easier to see in retrospect that this attitude, however idealistic it might have been, had within it the seeds of political isolationism that helped to bring about the rise of Hitler. By the time World War II broke out there were many who had begun to see this connection, but I believe that on the whole the American churches combined a high-minded religious pacifism with a diabolical political isolationism. Once the war began, the pressure to remain true to previously professed pacifist ideals was strong, and I recall considerable difficulty in this regard during my college years, which began precisely at the time of Hitler's invasion of Poland. I persisted in a pacifist position and applied for classification as a conscientious objector. Since I had indicated on my Selective Service forms that I expected to enter the ministry, my draft board classified me as a theological student. On the assumption that I would use my seminary training to prepare for reconstruction work after the war was over, I entered seminary the day after my college graduation.

During my time at Union Theological Seminary, however, a number of things happened to me. First of all, I got to know some students at Jewish Theological Seminary, directly across the street, and was thereby confronted in a more immediate way with what was happening in Europe. A number of these students had escaped from the Warsaw ghetto in 1938 or 1939 and had no idea what had happened to their parents or the rest of their families. Although firm data was hard to secure, it became clear that there were concentration camps, and that Hitler's anti-Semitic policy was being implemented in ghastly fashion. The impact of relationship with these Jewish students made clear to me that pacifism was at least not a technique that could be expected to "work" against a diabolical force like Nazism.

Another impact was the teaching of Reinhold Niebuhr, who helped me to distinguish between pacifism of witness and a pragmatic pacifism. He had high regard for the former, in which an individual simply said that he could not in conscience bear arms or kill. He had scant regard for the latter, which insisted (as I had been insisting up to that time) that pacifism could "win over" the recalcitrant opponent. While I believed then, and still believe, that pacifism can be an effective technique in many situations, particularly in individual and face-to-face encounters, it became increasingly clear that it was romanticism to assume that such an attitude could deflect the course of a tank or influence a bombing raid conducted from a height of thirty thousand feet.

A third factor was an increasing realization that my decision to do clean, creative reconstruction work after the war was dependent upon someone else doing the dirty, destructive work of destroying the power of Hitler so that the rest of us could do things that would not compromise our ideals.

The combination of these and other factors forced me to recognize that pacifism in that situation was a moral luxury that I could not afford. While I did not deny to others the right to engage in a pacifism of witness, I concluded that for me it was not a tenable position. I felt a moral obligation to be involved in the defeat of the forces of totalitarianism, and it seemed best to use my seminary training by entering the military chaplaincy, both to engage in a ministry to those in the armed forces and also to identify myself personally with their moral anguish. Thus, to the great dismay of my pacifist friends, immediately upon graduation I entered the Chaplains' Corps of the United States Navy and served on a troop transport in the Pacific Theater. Although my time in the service was relatively brief—and I have no heroic tales to recount—I saw Nagasaki and Bikini and a Jim Crow Navy, and no glorification of modern war will ever be a temptation to me.

After my discharge I remained in the Naval Reserve and lived through the cold war mentality of the 1950s and early '60s believing that the tragic choices open to us meant that the greatest ethical possibility lay in the precarious balance of terror that obtained during the period when only two great world powers had access to atomic weapons. Two things forced me to reassess that entire position: the civil rights struggle in the United States, and the U.S. military presence in Vietnam.

The introduction of nonviolence by Martin Luther King into the civil rights struggle initially struck me as an idealistic position that would bear no creative fruit. It was not long, however, before I saw the shallowness of that response and came to realize through Dr. King's words, and even more through his example, not only that nonviolence entailed a deep moral commitment but that it could also have significant pragmatic results. My own experience in some crisis situations during this period, a number of them in the deep South, convinced me that there was a significant possibility of changing the policies of our country through the practice of nonviolence. This conviction has been reinforced by the equally charismatic leadership of César Chavez in his long struggle, with Mexican-Americans, to achieve social justice through a similar commitment to nonviolence.

American involvement in Vietnam came hard on the heels of the engagement of many of our youth in the civil rights struggle. As a college professor, I found myself involved in their unwillingness to fight in an immoral war. To those who believed that our presence in Southeast Asia was profoundly wrong, it became important to protest that presence in as many ways as possible. For me this involved increasing commitment to students who were resisting the draft, and led finally to a willingness to engage in various types of civil disobedience on their behalf. (A fuller account of this pilgrimage is contained in the latter third of my book, *The Pseudonyms of God*, Westminster Press, 1972.)

While we were trying to protest violence abroad, it seemed to me crucial not to fuzz the issue by engaging in violence at home. Thus on both moral and pragmatic levels, I felt that resistance to our violent presence in Asia should be expressed through a nonviolent presence in America. The extraordinary unresponsiveness of both the Johnson and Nixon administrations to the anguished cries and actions of our youth led them, and on occasion me, to push further in the direction of symbolic acts of nonviolent protest that could register such protest adequately and still engage the support of thinking citizens.

This set of experiences has caused a rather agonizing reassessment of my own position on violence. Whereas I moved from nonviolence to support of violence in relation to World War II, in relation to civil rights and Vietnam I have moved in the opposite direction, toward a deeper and deeper commitment to nonviolence as a vehicle for producing social change.

It might be that the wheel would have come full circle, and that I would now be writing a book espousing nonviolence as the only possible option for religiously minded people, had there not been one further input to my thinking—one that will be evident in the pages that follow. This was my involvement, through a variety of ecumenical contacts in the latter part of the 1960s, with people from the "third world." I have discovered that many of my fellow Christians in Asia, Africa, and Latin America exist in such appalling political and economic oppression that for them the possibility of significant change by nonviolent means is scarcely entertainable. For them, nonviolence appears so ineffective as to put those who practice it on the side of oppression rather than liberation. They raise, therefore, a disturbing question about the overall efficacy of nonviolence as a means of producing social change.

But meeting them and reading some of their literature has done something even more important in raising my own level of consciousness as a relatively protected white American. For I have discovered from them that "violence" involves a great deal more than simply an overt physical act of destruction. It describes the *actual situation* of the great majority of the human family, whose existence is so exploited and demeaned (even though no overt physical actions are taking place) that they can indeed be described as victims of the continuing violence of our society, a violence for which, as I have already observed, white Americans bear a large measure of responsibility. Perhaps more than anything else, it is the implications of this discovery that forced me to write this book.

I have not come to the end of the road in pursuing those implications; but I have gone far enough to want to share some of the milestones that have appeared along the way.

CHAPTER ONE

Clarifying our Terms

It is, I think, a rather sad reflection on the present state of political science that our terminology does not distinguish among such key words as "power," "strength," "force," "authority," and, finally, "violence"—all of which refer to distinct, different phenomena and would hardly survive unless they did. . . . To use them as synonyms not only indicates a certain deafness to linguistic meanings, which would be serious enough, but it has also resulted in a kind of blindness to the realities they correspond to. In such a situation it is always tempting to introduce new definitions. . . .

Hannah Arendt, *On Violence*

IN THE FIELD OF THEOLOGY, as in political science, there is extraordinary confusion about both terms of our subject, *religion* and *violence*. Few words in our common vocabulary have been subject to greater abuse or misuse. Although we cannot hope to dispel all confusion, we can at least indicate some of the ways in which both words will be used in the pages that follow.

Religion in Dispute

Religion, for example, may be the supreme catchall or even the weasel word of our time. We are told glowingly about "the religion of America" in contrast to "the antireligion of godless communism," and are then subjected to a pejorative use of the word when a theologian makes the apparently paradoxical statement that "the Bible is the most antireligious book ever written" or a nontheologian announces that "religion is the opiate of the people."

A strong suspicion of the word *religion* in many theological circles stems in part from the attack leveled on it by Dietrich Bonhoeffer in the latter portion of his *Letters and Papers from Prison*. (Karl Barth, one of Bonhoeffer's mentors, had previously attacked religion as something that was "abolished" by Christianity.) Bonhoeffer, a German theologian, was imprisoned and subsequently executed by the Nazis for his part in the plot against Hitler's life. In his prison cell he speculated about the likelihood that we were entering into "a time of no religion at all," and began working on what he called a "nonreligious interpretation of Christianity." The project is available only in fragmentary form in the notes and letters smuggled past the prison censor, and it is possible to distinguish half a dozen meanings of the term as Bonhoeffer dissects it. Two of these are particularly noteworthy for our purposes.

One of them is Bonhoeffer's equation of religion with *metaphysics*, which he in turn defines as a dualistic approach to life in which there is another world at a far remove from our world. It is in this other world that God is to be found. Because he is a "stopgap" God, invoked to explain the things about our world that are still a mystery to us, he will become increasingly unnecessary as we understand our world more fully. We thus succeed in pushing him farther and farther out to the "edges" of life and live our lives more and more without recourse to him or need of him. He covers our residual ignorance, and the gradual elimination of our ignorance will lead to the gradual elimination of "the god of religion."

But Bonhoeffer also felt that men sought God in *inwardness* as well, in their own individual hearts or psyches, in a subjective way that did not involve God in the social dimension of human life. From this second perspective, God becomes "privatized," and religion becomes a matter of concern only to the individual and God. The neighbor and society can be conveniently overlooked.

When either of these understandings obtains—that God is either "out there" or "in here"—it is clear that religion so conceived has nothing of importance to contribute to an understanding of life, let alone such ongoing problems as violence.

There is no doubt that Bonhoeffer's analysis touched some raw nerve ends in our culture, and that much of our actual use of religion conforms to his description. To the degree that religion does, in fact, serve as a means of insulating us from the day-to-day problem of loving (or at least not destroying) our not-very-lovable neighbors, we can only applaud Bonhoeffer's intention and agree wholeheartedly with his strictures against what he calls "religion."

At the same time, there are good reasons for retaining the word itself. I wish it were possible to use another term, possibly *religiosity*, to describe the phenomenon Bonhoeffer abhors; for so deeply is the word *religion* embedded in our common experience and vocabulary, once the shock-value of Bonhoeffer's definitions has been appreciated, we are likely to become confused by ongoing references to religion in the world around us. But the word *will* remain, and there is no way to wish it out of existence.

There is a further reason why retention of the word *religion* will be useful in the subsequent discussion. It would have been possible to write about "Christianity and violence," or even "Protestantism and violence." Violence, however, is such a widespread reality in our world that this is surely not the time to fence ourselves off from one another in attempts to deal with it. We need the widest coalitions possible, and on the American scene it is particularly important that Protestants, Catholics, Jews, and "all men of goodwill" address themselves collectively to the problem. Thus while I inevitably see religion from the perspective of a Protestant Christian, and will not disavow whatever insights come to me from that tradition, I hope to write in such a way that representatives of the other traditions cited need not feel cut off from the discussion. (For a number of reasons, not least the limitations of space, I will not make extensive reference to the religions of the East, though a full-blown study would, of course, draw heavily on their contributions.)

With these caveats in mind let us look for a more positive meaning of the word *religion*. Although the etymology is itself in some dispute, there is agreement about a number of Latin roots from which our present word has come, and their convergent meanings are useful in seeking a working definition. The Latin *religare* refers to that which binds; *religio* refers to a constraint that no one can evade; and *religere* describes that which repeats itself, in the sense of a verdict to which we return again and again. The cumulative ingredients of these Latin terms, then, are the notion of a binding constraint from which we cannot escape, and to which we feel deeply committed.

These themes are helpfully drawn together in Paul Tillich's much-used and much-abused definition of religion as "ultimate concern." By this definition Professor Tillich meant that religion deals with that about which we are concerned in an ultimate way, that which we affirm with some kind of ultimate "seriousness" (to use another of his categories), or more simply, that in terms of which we live and for which we might even be willing to suffer or die. When we try to give *content* to this ultimate concern, we discover that there are many objects that men invest with ultimacy, many concerns that they hold with ultimate seriousness. We can approach our own individual existence with ultimate concern, for example, and demonstrate by our daily choice of priorities that nothing is more important to us than that; or we can invest our own nation with ultimacy, which is what we do when we say "My country right or wrong"; or we can do the same thing in relation to another person or a political ideology. It is worth pointing out that when we talk this way about "ultimates" we are really talking about what the word *god* has meant in human experience. As Martin Luther pointed out centuries ago, "That to which thy heart clings steadfastly, that truly is thy god." A contemporary example of the same point is provided by a recent symposium by a group of ex-communists; each tells the story of his commitment to the communist ideology and his subsequent disillusionment with the commitment that had assumed the nature of an "ultimate." The title of the published symposium is *The God That Failed*.

From this point of view, there are obviously few people who are truly "atheists," since an atheist would be someone with no ultimate concern at all. D. Mackenzie Brown quotes Professor Tillich:

> If people tell you, "I have no ultimate concern," which all of you have probably heard, then ask them, "Is there really nothing at all that you take with unconditional seriousness? What, for instance, would you be ready to suffer or even die for?" Then you will discover that even the cynic takes his cynicism with ultimate seriousness, not to speak of the others, who may be naturalists, materialists, communists, or whatever. They certainly take something with ultimate seriousness (*Ultimate Concern: Tillich in Dialogue*, p. 8).

The task then becomes one of discerning whether the objects invested with ultimacy are worthy of such allegiance. In the Old Testament, for example, the issue is seldom between those who believe in "God" and those who do not. The issue is rather that of commitment to *this* god or *that* one: does one give allegiance to the "God of Abraham, Isaac, and Jacob" or to the Baal of a Canaanite fertility cult? The real issue is not atheism but polytheism—the belief in many gods.

In these terms, religion involves our making a lasting commitment, choosing between a number of possible ultimate loyalties in a way that affects *all* that we are and do.

The latter point is important, and it is a point at which we can now reappropriate part of Bonhoeffer's polemic. He objected to any attempt to locate meaning exclusively outside the world or inside the individual. God, if he is truly God, must be found in the midst of everyday life, and at this point both he and Tillich are insisting on an emphasis that is driven home with great vigor in both the Judaic and Christian traditions. Jesus is simply drawing together two indivisible strains in Judaism when he indicates that the First Commandment, "You shall love the Lord your God with all your heart, mind, soul, and strength" (which is precisely what Tillich means by ultimate concern), is like unto the Second Commandment, "You shall love your neighbor as yourself" (which describes what Bonhoeffer means by being in the midst of life). The two commandments are simply two sides of the same coin; the way one expresses love for God is through the way one treats the neighbor. Few things could be more important in considering the relationship of religion and violence.

This Jewish strain in Jesus' teaching is likewise illustrated in the Parable of the Last Judgment (Matthew 25:31-46). Without becoming sidetracked by the difficult imagery of the parable, we can see that the main thrust is clear: when people are called upon to account for what they have done with their lives and how their ultimate concern has been expressed, the questions to which they must respond are not "Do you believe in God according to the proper creedal formulation?" or "Have you been properly baptized?" All the questions boil down to, simply, "What have you done for those in need?" There are specific queries about the hungry, the sick, the poor, the naked, the imprisoned. The depth of commitment to Christ is measured in terms of the depth of commitment to the neighbor.

We stated earlier that it was the *content* of the ultimate concern that made the difference. It should now be clear that the content presupposed as the word *religion* is used in the subsequent discussion is broader than the single tradition of Christianity but restrictive in the sense that it refers to what we usually describe as the Judeo-Christian tradition and the ways in which those within that tradition can join forces, in approaching the issue of violence, with all men of goodwill.

Conventional Definitions of Violence

In defining *religion*, our task was both to expand its meaning so that it could point to a reality in the life of all men, and also to reduce it so that we would not be talking about every manifestation of ultimate concern which is encountered but only about a few that could legitimately be grouped together.

In defining *violence*, however, we must move in a different direction, for the net result of the inquiry will be **to expand the meaning of the word far beyond our ordinary usage.** This is a risky business, since the wider a definition becomes, the more difficult it is to use it with precision. In this case, however, the risk is worth taking, because if violence is indeed more widespread than we usually acknowledge from white American perspectives, that fact is an important input for our subsequent treatment of it.

Our immediate response to the word *violence* is to think of it as describing an *overt physical act of destruction*: someone is roughed up, pushed around, hit, stabbed, shot, raped, or in some other way made the object of physical abuse. When such violence occurs, we can see it or feel it. This response is reinforced by many dictionaries. The initial definition in *Webster's Collegiate Dictionary* (fifth edition) describes violence as the "exertion of any physical force considered with reference to its effect on another than the agent." The initial definition of the adjective, *violent*, is similar: "moving, acting or characterized by *physical force*, especially by extreme and sudden or by unjust or improper force" (italics added).

The Eisenhower Commission which studied violence in America defined violence as "behavior designed to inflict physical injury to people or damage to property." Another conventional definition, offered by George Edwards as a foil for discussion in his book *Jesus and the Politics of Violence*, is: "Violence is physical force resulting in injury or destruction of property or persons in violation of general moral belief or civil law."

Richard Hofstadter, in his introduction to *American Violence: A Documentary History*, uses the term *violence* to describe those acts "which kill or injure persons or do significant damage to property." He illustrates the point by suggesting that force is being exerted when a line of policemen confronts demonstrators or strikers, and that "violence begins when they use their weapons."

These descriptions have the virtue of making instances of violence tangible and clear-cut. The question is not whether they are true as far as they go, but whether they go far enough. It is the thesis of this book that they do not, and that a great deal that might not strike white Americans as violence is nevertheless perceived as violence by a large part of the human family. It will therefore be worthwhile considering an expansion of the definition.

Beyond Conventional Definitions of Violence

An initial pointer toward an expanded definition can be found by noting that one of the Latin roots from which we get our English word is *violare*, which means "to violate." Whatever "violates" another, in the sense of infringing upon or disregarding or abusing or denying that other, whether physical harm is involved or not, can be understood as an act of violence. The basic overall definition of violence would then become *violation of personhood*. While such a denial or violation can involve the physical destruction of personhood in ways that are obvious, personhood can also be violated or denied in subtle ways that are not obvious at all, except to the victim. There can be "violation of personhood" quite apart from the doing of physical harm.

The term *personhood* is important. When we talk about a "person" we are not talking about an object but about a subject. We are describing someone who is not quantifiable or interchangeable with another. Each person has unique worth. There is no legitimate way to assert that one person is "worth more" than another person, since the worth of each is infinite. When Daniel Berrigan tells the violence-prone Weathermen that "no principle is worth the sacrifice of a single human life," he is attaching this high and unique value to personhood. And since personhood means the *totality* of the individual, and never just the body or just the soul, we are reinforced in our notion that violation of personhood can take place even when no overt physical harm is being done. In the broadest terms then, an act that depersonalizes would be an act of violence, since, as Simone Weil has suggested, it transforms a person into a thing.

Points on a Spectrum

Let us now examine some of the ways in which violation of personhood can take place. Professor Newton Garver has developed a helpful continuum along which we may position four manifestations of violence (Thomas Rose, ed., *Violence in America*, pp. 5-13).

1. The clearest instance of violence is, of course, *personal overt physical assault*, in which one person does physical harm to another.

2. When overt physical assault is practiced in corporate terms it becomes *institutionalized overt physical assault*. The clearest example is war: a society mobilizes its resources specifically for corporate acts of killing and destruction. This kind of violence is also present when a government maintains its own domestic power by a police force or army that liquidates the opposition through an ongoing reign of terror.

3. *Personal covert violence* takes place when one individual violates the personhood of another in ways that are psychologically destructive, rather than physically harmful. Professor Garver describes "the Freudian rebuff" as an example: an individual who expresses moral indignation over the Nazi concentration camps or the bombing of civilians in Vietnam is accused of projecting upon society an unhappy relationship with his father. When he protests such a characterization, he is accused of covering up his "real" reasons for outrage. Professor Garver's point is that there is absolutely no way to emerge from this kind of exchange with honor. The individual's dignity and personhood are denied when it is assumed beyond possibility of rebuttal that he is merely using his moral outrage about burning or bombing as a cover-up for deep-seated personal hang-ups he is unwilling to face.

4. Personal covert violence can become *institutionalized covert violence*. This occurs when the institutions or structures of society violate the personhood of society's members. Black children brought up in situations of substandard housing and inferior schooling, with consequent limitations of available job openings, are victims of institutionalized covert violence. It may be that no knives have been drawn, no blood has been shed, no bones have been broken, and yet the personhood of those children may have been violated to such a degree by the structures of their society that *violence* is an appropriate term to describe what has happened to them.

In our subsequent discussion we will not devote much attention to the overt forms of violence Professor Garver describes, except for a brief consideration of war as the most blatant of these. Our attention will focus mainly on what he calls "institutionalized covert violence" and which we will call "structured violence," which is the most difficult (and the most crucial) to discern in the contemporary world.

The Spiral of Violence

Dom Helder Camara, the Roman Catholic archbishop of Recife, Brazil, has offered an illuminating discussion of the *social* dimension of violence in a small book called *Spiral of Violence* (Dimension Books, 1971). To help us see more clearly the "hidden" character of the violence that surrounds us, we will draw upon his analysis in this section, even though we will illustrate his argument with material drawn from other sources. It is important to realize that Dom Helder lives in Brazil under one of the most repressive governments in the world, that he is a "revolutionary" in the sense that he feels there must be deep-seated social change, and that he also feels the change must be brought about nonviolently.

1. Dom Helder feels that the basic form of violence, which he calls Violence No. 1, is *injustice*. This is similar to what we have described as the hidden or covert violence that does not necessarily do direct physical harm, but is nonetheless a "violation of personhood." It is the subtle, institutionalized destruction of human possibilities that is around us all the time, but is often not apparent to those who are comfortably situated. It is present whenever the structures of society act so as to depersonalize and "thingify" people by making them objects rather than subjects.

Aristotle defined justice as "giving every man his due." John Bennett, former president of Union Theological Seminary, has offered an even better definition for our own day: "giving every child his due." When society is so organized that any child is deprived of those things he is entitled to have (food, clothing, education, for example), that society is unjust and is engaging in violence against the child.

This equation of violence and injustice is not one that has emerged only in recent times of acute social awareness; it is embedded even in the medieval philosophy of St. Thomas Aquinas. In his discussion of human law in *Summa Theologica*, Aquinas states that unjust laws "are acts of violence rather than laws." If a law is not derived from the eternal law, framed according to the proper use of reason, it is a wicked law, "and so, lacking the true nature of law, it is rather a kind of violence" (Ia, IIae, q. 96.4). There is a long history to the notion that injustice is "a kind of violence" and even an "act of violence."

President Johnson's Commission on the Causes and Prevention of Violence issued a report entitled *To Establish Justice, To Ensure Domestic Tranquillity*. While the report does not directly equate the terms *violence* and *injustice* as we are doing, it clearly recognizes that injustice breeds violence.

> The way in which we can make the greatest progress toward reducing [overt] violence in America is by taking the actions necessary to improve the conditions of family and community life for all who live in our cities, and especially for the poor who are concentrated in the ghetto slums. . . . To make violence unnecessary, our institutions must be capable of providing justice for all who live under them. . . . Violence has usually been the lava flowing from the top of a volcano fed by deeper fires of social dislocation and injustice; it has not been stopped solely by capping the top, but has usually subsided when our political and social institutions have managed to make the adjustments necessary to cool the fires below.

2. When the injustice of society becomes too oppressive, Violence No. 2, which Dom Helder calls *revolt*, bursts forth. Those who have been the victims of injustice finally decide that they must throw off the shackles of their oppression and end the massive injustice they have suffered. This is the kind of violence with which the Presidential Commission is chiefly concerned, "the lava flowing from the top of a volcano fed by deeper fires of social dislocation and injustice." Such violence usually involves physical destructiveness, sometimes on a massive scale, depending on the number and efficiency of those who revolt. Violence as revolt is directed against the status quo, against those who have the power and are responsible for the injustice, by those who feel that they have been denied power and justice and personhood.

One of the clearest justifications of violence as revolt is the following statement, set in the context of a discussion of the ends for which true government exists:

> Whenever any form of government becomes destructive of these ends, it is *the right of the people to alter or to abolish it*, and to institute new government, laying its foundation on such principles and organizing its powers in such form as to them shall seem most likely to effect their safety and happiness. . . . When a long train of abuses and usurpations, pursuing invariably the same object, evinces a design to reduce them under absolute despotism, *it is their right, it is their duty, to throw off such government* and to provide new guards for their future security.

To most readers, this quotation (with its power-to-the-people emphasis indicated by the italicized portions) sounds like something straight out of *The Communist Manifesto*, the collected writings of Karl Marx, or a speech from some third-world revolutionary. Such a guess would be close, for it is taken from the Black Panther Party Program statement of March 29, 1972. But the guess would not be close enough, for what the Black Panthers did was simply to appropriate as their own a number of sentences from the Declaration of Independence of the United States of America, in which, on July 4, 1776, the theme of the right of revolt was described as a "self-evident truth." Responding to a situation of injustice, the founding fathers asserted that revolt was an appropriate response, and it will be important to bear this in mind when we turn to examine contemporary revolutionary movements inspired by the same motivation. Violence as revolt, then, takes place when injustice has reached the place where a large group of people will no longer bear it passively or silently. Thomas Rose is only fortifying Dom Helder's point when he comments, "The basic cause of most violent revolt is injustice and inequity, violation of personhood, and symbolic violence" (*Violence in America*, p. 38).

3. Just as Violence No. 1 (injustice) leads to Violence No. 2 (revolt), so does Violence No. 2 lead to Violence No. 3, which Dom Helder calls *repression*. Confronted with revolt, those who hold power put down the revolt by whatever repressive means are necessary to ensure that their power is not threatened.

In the face of the revolt, token concessions by those in power are sometimes sufficient to defuse the revolt and persuade the revolters that they have achieved sufficient gains. This is what Herbert Marcuse calls "repressive tolerance"; a tiny spearhead of revolt will be legitimized within the system, and certain expressions of revolt will be tolerated so long as they are kept within clearly defined boundaries. But the "tolerance" is "repressive" since no widespread change is allowed.

This is close to the position taken by Messrs. Nixon, Agnew, and Mitchell in relation to antiwar demonstrators in 1970; the public was assured that "dissent" was indeed part of "the American way," but administration spokesmen made clear that dissent must not really change anything (e.g., stop the war) and that policy makers would be unmoved by the substantive concerns of the dissenters. At the same time governmental orders went out to crack down on dissenters. Similarly, there is a significant degree of freedom of the press in South Africa today, and the English-speaking press is strongly critical of the government's policy of *apartheid*, often courageously so. But since the English-speaking population is only a fraction of the voting population, the government can afford to tolerate dissent because it does not truly threaten the status quo.

I add one personal example of the subtle form of repression that a government can exercise. In 1967 two polite and soft-spoken men came to my office, flashed their badges, and informed me that they were checking on my antiwar activities for the FBI. They were trying to collect information from me and my friends that could be used as a basis for bringing criminal charges against me. The demeanor was sophisticated and suave, but behind it was a clear threat that was less sophisticated and suave. The threat was that if I did not cease doing what I was doing, I would end up in jail. I could not help but interpret this as a "violation of my personhood" since I was being told to stop doing what in conscience I felt compelled to do, or let the FBI take direct control of my life.

If subtle ways of acting repressively are insufficient, those with power are always prepared to act more openly and destructively. Dom Helder lives in a country where there is a constant escalation of repressive tactics against those who oppose the government. He himself has been denied the right to speak over the radio and several attempts have been made on his life. His priests have been arrested, and many of his countrymen have been imprisoned and tortured, either to exact information or to serve as object lessons to others the government wishes to frighten.

In any country, concern for "law and order" can represent a legitimate desire to maintain a sufficient structure in society so that looting or random destructiveness can be avoided, but the same concern can also become an extraordinarily effective instrument of repression, invoked whenever there is the slightest danger that the status quo might be challenged. Laws themselves can be unjust (as we have already learned from Aquinas), and the invoking of an unjust law can help to maintain injustice and act as a force of repression.

We see increasing examples of this kind of repression in the United States. The repression does not come in the form of storm troopers kicking Jews in the gutters, but in the more subtle form of widespread erosion of the right of dissent and increasingly repressive measures against those who persist in dissent. The clearest recent symbol of this sort of repression was the government's attempt to convict a small group of pacifist nuns and priests of conspiracy to blow up federal buildings in Washington and kidnap Henry Kissinger. The government built its case on the testimony of a paid informer who infiltrated the group and acted as an *agent provocateur*. The informer, who had operated under a dozen aliases and had a long history of lying, was not able to convince a "middle-America" jury of the truth of his claims, even though the administration spent over $1 million on the case. The intimidations that flow from such government-initiated attempts to discredit and destroy responsible dissent are frightening. (For further details, see Raines, ed., *Conspiracy: The Implications of the Harrisburg Trial for the Democratic Tradition*, Harper and Row, 1973.)

It is this sequence from injustice to revolt to repression that Dom Helder calls the "spiral of violence." And the spiral continues as repression breeds even greater injustice, which in turn invokes more militant revolt, thereby leading to uglier repression than before.

Where do we Start?

How do we stop the spiral? It becomes clear that the point at which we usually focus our attention and moral outrage is Violence No. 2, revolt. This is where we see the threat to the order, peace, and stability of society. When there is a race riot, for example, we ask plaintively why the people in Watts or Detroit do not act nonviolently. We insist that they are wrong to try to make their point by burning and looting, and since they nevertheless engage in violent revolt, we find ample reason to justify repression (Violence No. 3) as the only appropriate way to put down their revolt (Violence No. 2). It is this syndrome, as we have seen, that has been reflected in the rhetoric and action of both the Johnson and Nixon administrations in their increasingly strong-arm methods of quelling dissent.

But surely this misses the point. The place to focus attention is not on Violence No. 2, revolt, but on the *basic cause* of that violence, which is (as Dom Helder reminds us) found in Violence No. 1, injustice. It is because of the injustices of our society that the spiral of violence initially gets launched, and until and unless we get at the roots of injustice, we will be dealing in only a superficial way with the problem of violence. As Dom Helder puts it, "The only true answer to violence is to have the courage to face the injustices which constitute Violence No. 1."

That is the hardest lesson for white Americans to learn. It may also be the most important.

CHAPTER TWO

War as the Most Obvious Example of Violence

The peculiarity of war is not its violence. The seemingly normal society embodies more violence than is usually apparent. The peculiar problem of war is that it represents magnified violence between states or factions unrestrained by government.
Roger Shinn, *Wars and Rumors of Wars*

WE HAVE ALREADY SEEN THAT VIOLENCE, in the form of injustice, is found in unexpected places; and we have suggested that its presence is more pervasive than we normally realize. It will be easier to detect violence in its subtle form if we first of all observe it in its blatant form. As the above quotation indicates, war "represents magnified violence"; violence when all the bars are down, when not even governments can restrain the combatants. The relationship between religion and violence, therefore, can be explored in a preliminary way if we look at various religious attitudes toward war.

Biblical Views of Warfare and Violence

There is a great deal about warfare and violence in the writings that have nourished our Western culture, the Old and New Testaments. If anything emerges with clarity after an examination of their contents, it is that no single viewpoint dominates the great variety of writings that comprise the Jewish and Christian Scriptures. The Devil, as has been pointed out many times, can quote Scripture for his purposes, and in no area of our experience, perhaps, has this been truer than in the uses to which Scripture has been put in justifying or condemning war.

We must first guard against an oversimplification that often intrudes in Christian circles, to the effect that the God of the Old Testament is a God of warfare and vengeance, while the God of the New Testament is a God of love and peace. This is one of those polemical generalizations that will not hold up under even the most superficial scrutiny. To be sure, there are bloodthirsty passages in the old Testament—a fact that should not be surprising, considering the historical context out of which many of those passages came into being. We find the psalmist, for example, saying, "Happy shall be he who takes your little ones and dashes them against the rock!" (Psalm 137:9), and we find Saul being castigated because after a particular battle he did *not* follow the divine command to "slay all the men, women, and children of the Amalekites."

But if there are passages like these, there are also passages that witness to the surpassing tenderness of God's love for his people, and the peace that he will bring. Here is the prophet Isaiah:

> They shall beat their swords into plowshares, and their spears into pruning hooks, nation shall not lift up sword against nation, neither shall they learn war any more (Isaiah 2:4; see also Micah 4:3).

Few pictures of a world at peace are more exalted than that contained later in Isaiah:

> The wolf shall dwell with the lamb, and the leopard shall lie down with the kid, and the calf and the lion and the fatling together, and a little child shall lead them. The cow and the bear shall feed; their young shall lie down together; and the lion shall eat straw like the ox. The suckling child shall play over the hole of the asp, and the weaned child shall put his hand on the adder's den. They shall not hurt nor destroy in all my holy mountain; for the Earth shall be full of the knowledge of the Lord as the waters cover the sea (Isaiah 11:6-9).

Another crucial emphasis in the Old Testament is the stress on the *justice* of God, a justice that is combined with mercy. The universe has a moral character, according to the Old Testament writers, which insures that in the end those who commit injustice will be brought low. Again and again the prophets inveigh against injustice, and when its excesses become sufficiently exacerbating, injustice is always challenged and God is found to be on the side of the oppressed. Condemnation is not reserved for those who commit violence against injustice, but for those who are the architects of the injustice that makes committing violence necessary.

In the New Testament there are various attitudes as well. John the Baptist does not tell soldiers to go AWOL; he merely urges them not to grumble about their wages. Jesus says, "I have not come to bring peace, but a sword" (Matthew 10:34), which even though it may be only a metaphor is nevertheless a particularly military metaphor. He further says, "If my kingdom were of this world, my servants would fight" (John 18:36). There is no clearly recorded opposition on Jesus' part to the fact that some of his disciples took swords when they went to the Garden of Gethsemane, although he told Peter, when that impetuous follower used his sword against a soldier, "All who take the sword will perish by the sword" (Matthew 26:52).

But even if we take such scattered verses as these and add to them the incident of Jesus clearing the money-changers out of the temple, the overall picture that emerges clearly puts the burden of proof on those who would use Jesus' life or teachings in order to justify going to war. Not only is it wrong to *kill* the enemy—even *hating* the enemy is proscribed. There is a positive command to love the enemy and even to pray for him. He may not be the subject of retaliation; if one is smitten on the cheek, the other cheek must be turned. It is not the warmakers who are blessed, but the peacemakers (see the summary of Jesus' teaching in Matthew 5-7). The prevailing viewpoint seems clear.

Even St. Paul, who must have had a more choleric disposition than Jesus, sounds much the same. Paul quotes the Hebrew Scriptures:

> Bless those who persecute you; bless and do not curse them. . . . Live in harmony with one another. . . . Repay no one evil for evil, but take thought for what is noble in the sight of all. If possible, so far as depends on you, live peaceably with all. Beloved, never avenge yourselves, but leave it to the wrath of God; for it is written, "Vengeance is mine, I will repay, says the Lord." If your enemy is hungry, feed him; if he is thirsty, give him drink; for by so doing you will heap burning coals upon his head. Do not be overcome by evil, but overcome evil with good (Romans 12:14-21).

Even with this kind of evidence, however, we cannot make a simplistic transfer of the New Testament materials to our own time. There are at least two reasons for this. First, it is undeniable that both Jesus and Paul expected an imminent end to history; they felt that God was about to intervene and establish his kingdom, and that the present world situation of the Christian was going to be of relatively short duration (although Paul gradually modified his views and began to deal with the Church's problem of preparing for a long-term future on earth). Secondly, there is the further complication that recent New Testament studies make it more difficult to determine precisely what Jesus' own attitude was toward the "revolutionary movements" at work in his day. It is somewhat surprising to learn that one and possibly two of the twelve apostles were Zealots, members of a revolutionary group dedicated to overthrowing the Roman government by force. An extended literature has grown up around the problem of Jesus' attitude toward the Zealots; scholars such as Brandon have even suggested that there was a conspiracy of silence in the gospels so that the early Church would not get into further trouble with Rome as a politically subversive movement. The results of the investigation, however, while they challenge a simplistic identification of Jesus with pacifism, do not justify the notion that he can be transformed into an advocate of violent revolution.

Three Basic Attitudes in Christian History

Supporting the notion that Jesus bequeathed his followers a legacy of opposition to violence and warfare is the fact that, of the three basic positions on war that emerged in Christian history, the earliest was an unequivocal *pacifism*. The early Christians, who took very seriously the injunction that they were not to take up the sword, refused to serve in Roman armies for several centuries. Early literature gives ample evidence of the pacifist position of the Christian Church.

Later on, when the peace and stability of the Roman Empire were threatened by the invasion of barbarians from the north, Christians began to argue that there might be times when they could be justified in waging war, if certain specified criteria were met. This position came to be called the doctrine of *the just war*, and we shall shortly examine it. A third position that emerged still later was the theory of *the holy war* or *crusade*, which involved an acceptance of whatever kind of force or violence was necessary to secure a given end, and the unquestioning participation of the Christian on the assumption that God's will was being served.

Although the latter position is seldom advanced by responsible church leaders today, it is frequently echoed in the public rhetoric of politicians—Mr. Nixon's reference to America's presence in Vietnam as one of our shining hours being only a single case in point. The options of pacifism and the just war, however, have persisted throughout Christian history and have increasingly influenced contemporary thinking, particularly in relation to the formulation of a position on conscientious objection to war. It will be helpful to look more closely at both of them, since they focus on some of the issues of the overall question of religion and violence that will occupy us in subsequent chapters.

Criteria for a Just War

One of the most interesting developments in recent theology has been the revival of the "just war" theory. This position was developed by St. Augustine (in response to the circumstances cited above), given careful treatment by St. Thomas Aquinas in the medieval period, and further refined by the Jesuit theologian Suárez during the Counter-Reformation. It subsequently fell into disrepute largely because any war being waged by the country in which a proponent of the theory resided invariably turned out to be a "just war"—a situation that has changed only in recent years, as we shall presently see.

There are at least six criteria by reference to which a war might be denominated "just":

1. The war must be *declared by a legitimate authority*; it must not be the expression of a private grudge of an individual or group of individuals who simply decide to throw their weight around. During most of the time the just war theory has operated, "declaration by a legitimate authority" has meant declaration by a prince or sovereign head of state.

2. The war must be *carried out with a right intention*; its purpose must be to promote peace. This is simply a spelling out of the basic natural law theory in ethics, that good should be promoted and evil avoided. The war must be carried out with the intention that good shall result rather than evil, that peace and justice will follow rather than tyranny. A war cannot be just if it is waged with a wrong intention, such as the desire to secure vengeance or to satisfy lust for domination.

3. The war must be undertaken *only as a last resort*. No war can be just as long as there is *any* chance of resolving the conflict by discussion, negotiation, the employment of economic sanctions, or other means short of military action. All means for a peaceful solution must

have been exhausted before resort to military force can be justified.

4. The war must be waged on the basis of *the principle of proportionality*. The relationship between ends and means must be proportionate; i.e., there cannot be excessive destruction for the sake of even minimally desirable ends. The good to be accomplished must outweigh the evil that will be exercised in bringing about the good.

5. The war must have *a reasonable chance of success*. This is not a cynical provision but a moral consideration, for unless there is a good chance that the objective for waging war can be achieved, it is immoral to incur the damage and destruction that will result.

6. The war must be waged *with all the moderation possible*. Clear codes of conduct in time of war have emerged, embodied in internationally accepted rules of warfare endorsed by the Hague Convention, the Geneva Convention, and other such bodies. It is never legitimate to go beyond the minimal moral constraints that have been agreed upon. Wanton violence is prohibited; so is looting; so are massacres. Particular care must be taken to see that civilian noncombatants and prisoners of war are not tortured or killed. The criterion has reference not only to the actual hostilities, but also to the terms of settlement at the end of the war—terms that must embody charity and justice rather than vengeance.

Father John Coleman, S.J., has noted certain important things about the application of these criteria: (a) The presumption in "just war" theory is always *against* war, not in favor of it. There is no attempt to glorify war or to make it seem less evil than it is. The burden of proof is always upon the one who would wage war, and *all* of the criteria must be met if the war is to be called "just." (b) The criteria remain operative *during* the waging of the war. A war originally undertaken for just cause could be waged so unjustly that continuing participation in it might have to be condemned. Most Christians, for example, felt that the initiation of war against Nazism was just, but many were increasingly troubled by the obliteration bombing of German cities, the imposition of unconditional surrender, and the American use of atomic weapons in Japan. Such actions increasingly called into question the justness of the Allied cause. (c) Since the presumption is always against war, there is a built-in presumption in support of dissent from participation in war. The principle that certain wars could be just carries with it the corollary that other wars might be unjust. It would follow that an individual could participate in a just war but not in an unjust war. Without calling himself an absolute pacifist, he could still insist on the right to "selective conscientious objection" to a particular war if it did not meet the criteria that would allow for conscientious participation.

Applying the Just War Theory Today: A Case Study

Setting out criteria for a just war is not merely an intellectual exercise. There are at least two important ways in which it can further our understanding of violence.

First of all, the criteria have potential transfer value from the isolated case of overt violence in war to the overall case of covert violence in society; we can employ them to help determine whether there might be cases in which it would conceivably be just to use physical violence as a remedy for the hidden violence present in unjust social structures. Might there, in other words, be such a thing as a just revolution? (This issue will be discussed in Chapter 5.)

Secondly, we can apply the criteria to a specific war in order to see whether they provide any significant moral leverage for reaching a decision about its justness or lack of justness. Since the war in Vietnam has been the most recent instance of American military involvement, and since it provides a model of what future American wars might be like, we will use it as a case study. As suggested earlier, the use of just war criteria in the past has always worked out to justify the particular war under scrutiny. In relation to Vietnam, however, this pattern has not obtained. The following comments are not merely my own reflections, but a summary of considerable discussion among moral theologians.

1. It is clear that the war in Vietnam did not meet the criterion of being *declared by a legitimate authority*, since it was never declared at all. Not only was there no formal declaration of war, but the actual *de facto* prosecution of the war was implemented by the executive branch of the American government rather than the legislative branch. Since only the legislative branch of the government is empowered to declare war, it is seriously argued by some legal experts that the extended American military presence in Vietnam was unconstitutional.

2. Similar questions can be raised about the second criterion, that the war be *carried out with a right intention*. Whatever may have been the public rhetoric of the policy makers about their intentions in waging the war (i.e., to bring about peace and avoid evil), the publication of the Pentagon Papers has shown that many other motivations were at work and that there was deliberate duplicity on the part of elected and appointed government officials. Even if there had been an initial right intention in sending a small group of military advisors to Vietnam, the escalation of that presence to half a million ground troops by Mr. Johnson, and the transformation of that presence to the most intensive bombing raids in human history by Mr. Nixon, render invalid any ongoing claim to a right intention.

3. The third criterion, that a war can be undertaken *only as a last resort* when all peaceful means of solution have been exhausted, is likewise rendered dubious by the history of American presence. In the years of gradually escalating American military power in Vietnam, there were numerous instances of peace initiatives from Hanoi, all of which were met by increased American military escalation rather than a willingness to negotiate. (See Schurmann, Scott, and Zelnik, *The Politics of Escalation in Vietnam,* Beacon Press, 1966.) Even in 1972, during highly pressured peace negotiations by Henry Kissinger, American bombing was *increased* rather than decreased, and amid talk of a cease-fire there was an increasing buildup of American military supplies to South Vietnam. Throughout the years of American presence, war has been a first resort, rather than a last resort.

4. Perhaps the most grossly violated of the criteria for a just war is the fourth, *the principle of proportionality.* Each day the destructiveness of the war continued it became more difficult to assert that the good resulting from the American presence would outweigh the evil inflicted on the country by that presence. The violation of the criterion is epitomized by the famous comment of an Army colonel at the time of the capture of the pile of rubble that had once been Ben Tre: "We had to destroy the city in order to save it." The argument that American military might was needed to forestall the bloodbath that would occur in the wake of a communist takeover was more than offset by the ongoing bloodbath that American military power indiscriminately inflicted on the entire country and its inhabitants. By no conceivable moral calculus can it be argued that the good accomplished by American power justified the evil entailed. We have been willing to destroy a *country* in order to "save" it.

5. The criterion that the war must have *a reasonable chance of success* might initially have had some appeal, but the history of the war made the argument increasingly dubious. Even Mr. Johnson discovered that it was not possible to "bomb Hanoi to its knees," and hundreds of thousands of lives could have been saved if Mr. Nixon had realized that intensive air raids served to stiffen the morale of the North Vietnamese rather than to weaken it. Many who pursue the argument believe that the "peace terms" announced in October of 1972 were certainly no more favorable to the United States than those that could have been secured four years earlier—which, if true, leads to the unanswered question of why it was necessary to prolong brutal destruction for four more years. And none of these comments gets to the heart of the question: by what conceivable standard can the long-range destructiveness of the war be described as a "success"?

6. All of the previous discussion comes to a focus in the final criterion, that the war must be waged *with all the moderation possible.* This is not a conceivable standard to apply to the Vietnam war, whether one is talking about the intensity of destruction (more bombs dropped than in any other war in human history), the widespread devastation (defoliation of crops and jungles, destruction of unprotected villages), the slaughter of civilians (extensive use of napalm, guava bombs, and other antipersonnel weapons), or the disregard of every one of the "laws of international warfare" that are legally binding on the American nation (torture of prisoners, many counterparts of the My Lai massacre).

It may turn out that this erosion of moral constraint, and the increasing disregard of the principle of moderation, will be the most devastating legacy of the Vietnam war.

It is obvious that the above discussion is compressed and only suggestive. More data would be necessary to make the case convincing to the as yet unconvinced. All that is necessary for the purposes of the present argument is to see that the criteria of the just war can raise grave doubts about the justness of the American participation in the war in Vietnam. A conclusion that the war cannot be justified by these criteria will not undo the damage that has been done in Southeast Asia, but it might at least post flag warnings against similar American military involvement in other parts of the world in the future.

A Critique of the Just War Theory

The above discussion offers a fairly optimistic view of the uses to which the doctrine of the just war can be put. It is therefore important to note some of the limitations of the just war theory.

One of these has already been suggested: until recent times, proponents of a just war theory have invariably been able to justify any wars in which their own nations were involved, suggesting that the theory has the built-in danger of being no more than a self-serving device. A second problem is that the nations (or, in the past, the monarchs) serve as judges in their own case. Who is to say that all legitimate alternatives have been exhausted before war is declared? Presumably only the ones who have tried them out and had access to sufficient information to make intelligent decisions on the matter. Once again, self-serving rationalization can enter in. It will be remembered that in the early days of the escalation of the Vietnam war public questioning was always countered with the insistence that only "the experts" knew enough to be able to make decisions.

The most sustained recent attack on the just war theory is offered by James Douglass, a Roman Catholic pacifist, in *The Non-Violent Cross*. While Douglass's response is directed chiefly against the particular version of the just war theory espoused by Paul Ramsey, the points he makes deserve thoughtful attention. He believes that the just war theory has too many loopholes, and as a consequence its proponents can always find a rationale for supporting war. Christians, he feels, must be so transformed that "conscience will not only be purged of the nuclear sword but reformed in the strength of the nonviolent cross." He feels that "a morally limited war has already been excluded from possibility in the Nuclear Age," and that any just war theory that can countenance nuclear warfare has demonstrated its moral bankruptcy, and has, however imperceptibly, given its sanction to total war. The components of just war theory do not seem to him strong enough to withstand the pressures to support a nuclear war. The notion of "justifying" from a Christian perspective "25 million discriminately dead" (as the result of a preemptive air strike) against the prospect of "215 million indiscriminately dead" (if a major power launches an attack to which another power responds) strikes Douglass (and me) as grotesque.

I do not believe, however, that the version of the just war expounded above and the position espoused by Douglass are at a far remove from one another, even though he proceeds from an absolute pacifist position and I do not. The logic of the just war position in the nuclear age seems to me to come very close to Douglass's own position. I can come close to accepting his own statement of the terms under which a just war theory could possess moral integrity:

> To preserve its own integrity in the Nuclear Age, the just war doctrine demands of the nation the cross of unilateral disarmament—and if the nation refuses [which I believe it will—R.M.B.] it demands of the individual the cross of conscientious objection. Unless the just war doctrine can support a stand in conscience against all war in the Nuclear Age, whether it be the savagery of counterrevolutionary warfare or the global suicide of thermonuclear war, the doctrine is revealed as a de facto capitulation to total war (*The Non-Violent Cross*, p. 171).

The point of difference comes, I believe, at whether it is an *a priori* truth that an internal revolution, seeking to overthrow an unjust regime, will escalate into "total war." Vietnam is strong evidence that it may, since America's intervention led to destruction so massive that any distinction between it and total war is a semantic subtlety surely lost upon the Vietnamese victims. It has not, however, led to a total war in a global sense. It is conceivable that America may have learned a lesson from its disastrous intervention—a lesson from which other world powers might also learn—though it will require the utmost public vigilance to keep that lesson in mind when revolutionary forces in some other small country threaten the stability of American interests there.

Pacifism as a New Possibility

It is not only James Douglass who sees pacifism as the true moral possibility for our time. The witness of many others, symbolized by the Berrigan brothers and their friends on the "Catholic left," is indicative of what may become an increasing commitment, particularly among the young. Many have been pushed toward pacifism as they have explored what it would mean to participate in the Vietnam war, and have come to the conclusion that participation in such a war would be morally reprehensible. Furthermore, they have come to see Vietnam not simply as one unfortunate exaggeration of the nature of modern warfare, but as a wholly typical example of what warfare is likely to be in the future. An examination of the morality of the Vietnam war persuades them that similar standards of morality will obtain in all future wars—that moral constraints will again be eroded to the vanishing point so that the only possible reply to the demand to participate in a future war must be a resounding "no."

The position is further buttressed by the disastrous side effects of modern war. Those who say no to modern war see that a nation putting its industry, economy, and manpower into a war inevitably neglects using those resources to combat racism, urban blight, and unequal opportunities for education, as national priorities become increasingly distorted. They see war as a laboratory in which technicians experiment at human expense with new devices for human destruction, from napalm and white phosphorus bombs to automated battlefields. They see the mood of wartime as one that threatens the legitimacy of dissent and thereby erodes the democratic process, and they can point to any number of utterances by Messrs. Johnson, Humphrey, Nixon, and Agnew to make their point. They see Americans perturbed as white-skinned soldiers die, but increasingly unperturbed as dark-skinned soldiers and civilians die. In short, the cumulative impact of modern warfare, far from the battlefield as well as on it, only reinforces their conviction that they have passed the point of no return in relation to support of warfare.

They are, in other words, very close to the position of the early

Church, even though they have arrived there by a different route. Pacifism, which may once have seemed idealistic and unrealistic as a human stance, looks increasingly like the most hardheaded and realistic position imaginable when one looks at war as the most obvious example of violence.

Moving from the Most Obvious Example
to Less Obvious Ones

But there is a further conclusion to be drawn from our examination of war, and it serves as a transition to the argument of the pages that follow. When we look at war as "the most obvious example of violence," we are reminded more forcefully than ever of the *less* obvious examples of violence that surround us whether we are in the midst of war or not. We have come to see the war in Vietnam not as one cruel and stupid blunder in the ongoing life of a society that is otherwise acceptable, but as an extreme example of what continues to be wrong in a society that is unacceptable and must be changed. Our callousness toward dark-skinned deaths in Vietnam is a reminder of our callousness toward dark-skinned lives in America. Our attempt to force a small country into submission in Asia is a reminder of our attempt to force small groups (Indians, Puerto Ricans, Chicanos) into submission here at home. Our willingness to spend over $60 billion every year on defense is a reminder of our unwillingness to spend less than $6 billion over several years, as recommended by the Kerner Commission report, to reverse the racist direction of our domestic life. In these and a dozen other examples that could be offered, violence, as violation of personhood, is taking place all the time. The violence that takes place in war is only an exaggerated reminder of the violence that takes place in the rest of our society.

This leads us to the uncomfortable conclusion that we will not have *disposed* of the problem of violence in our society once we have disposed of the problem of war. We will only have *exposed* the problem for what it is, a problem that is widespread and pervasive in all aspects of our society. We must turn therefore from the issue of war, as the most obvious example of violence in our society, and concentrate our attention on the more subtle and hidden forms of violence that constitute the real problem.

CHAPTER THREE

Broadening our View of the Problem: The Continuing Reality of Violence in Society

Violence, less and less embarrassed by the limits imposed by centuries of lawfulness, is brazenly and victoriously striding across the whole world.

Alexander Solzhenitsyn, in his
Nobel Prize acceptance speech

THE NEED TO LOOK BEYOND the violence represented by war to the reality of violence in society is symbolized in a dilemma stated by Helmut Gollwitzer, a German theologian. Unwilling to fight for Hitler in World War II, Professor Gollwitzer went into the Medical Corps of the German Army, was captured by the Russians, and spent five years in a POW camp in Russia. He emerged from this set of experiences as a nuclear pacifist, convinced that the perils of nuclear warfare are so great that the only Christian option remaining is that of pacifism. But, as he discovered at the Prague Peace Conference:

... just at this moment when we ... are inclined to regard as mistaken the traditional approval of Christian participation in the use of military force, and hoist the flag of pacifism ... We hear from our brethren in the underdeveloped countries (where the situation is a revolutionary one) that they consider it incumbent upon them to participate in national and social revolutionary struggles which involve the use of force (Marty and Peerman, eds., *New Theology No. 6*, p. 113).

Although he sees clearly the importance of a pacifist position in relation to war, Professor Gollwitzer has discovered that when the issue is not world war but rather a revolutionary struggle for human dignity, those involved in the struggle see pacifism or nonviolence as a moral cop-out. In the light of this conviction, and its implications for many other churchmen, it is important to broaden the problem by looking at the reality of violence in our society. We can do this through four interconnected propositions.

1. We Live in a Revolutionary Situation

This may appear far from self-evident to most white Americans, but it is increasingly self-evident not only to many nonwhite Americans but to more and more non-Americans, whether white or not. We will see this even more clearly in the next chapter when we listen to the views of the non-Americans.

For a number of years it was customary to speak in ecumenical circles of the phenomenon of rapid social change in such parts of the world as Africa, Asia, and Latin America. It is now clear that rapid social change is a euphemism for revolution, and the revolution is far more widespread than most white Americans want to contemplate. It is a revolution in which the very structures that have defined the good society (as middle-class people have known it) are being challenged and threatened either as unworkable or as hypocritical facades designed to help those already in power remain entrenched in power. At issue are some of our commonly held assumptions: the belief that the polling booth is a place in which the will of the majority is expressed for the good of all; the belief that in a mobile society anyone who works hard enough can get to the top; the conviction that police power is exercised in a disinterested attempt to see that justice prevails; the assumption that elected officials act on behalf of all their constituents. These and similar assertions draw only derisive sneers from increasingly large numbers of the human family. To them, democratic structures are rigged in favor of the "haves" and against the "have-nots"; only those who have the right connections and the right skin color can hope to "get to the top"; the police are a supreme symbol of repression; politicians cater to those who pay them off. When one moves from democratic structures (which do not look so democratic to the dispossessed) to authoritarian ones, the discrepancies between promise and performance are even more blatant.

Consider these facts about the world in which we live:

- An average of 15,000 people starve to death *every day*.
- Two-thirds of the human family go to bed hungry each night—and many of those do not even have beds.
- Twenty percent of the people of the world control eighty percent of the world's resources.
- In 1970 the *increase* over the previous year in the gross national product in the United States was greater than the *entire* gross national product of the continent of Africa. Americans had more for luxuries than Africans had for everything.

(For further extensive data, see Bryant, *A World Broken by Unshared Bread*, World Council of Churches, 1970, as well as publications of the Commission on Society, Development and Peace, Geneva.)

The issues are further sharpened when the racial component is introduced; it is a white-skinned minority of the human family that has most of the world's goods and power, and a dark-skinned majority that is almost universally deprived of a fair share of either goods or power.

On a global scale as well as on a domestic scale, there is an increasing unwillingness to accept this inequity lying down. Those who feel themselves victimized are determined to be victimized no longer. Such inequity breeds rapid social change—or, as we had better become accustomed to saying, revolution. The deprived, particularly as they realize that they are the majority, will not tolerate deprivation indefinitely. Having long been denied power, they are more and more determined to seize power if it is not voluntarily given to them.

2. The Fundamental Question Is One of Power: Violence or Nonviolence Is a Subordinate Question of Means

What is fundamentally at stake in the revolutionary situation is the question of the use of power: Who has it? How is it exercised? For what ends?

The World Council of Churches Consultation on Racism at Notting

Hill in 1969 stated that the key issue was "not simply that of violence versus nonviolence, but the use of power for the powerful and the need of power for the powerless." Ulrich Scheuner underlines the issue:

> The really decisive question is not the question of violence—especially since the concept of "violence" can be widened to cover indirect forms of pressure—but the question of the justification for the use of power, the consequent limits of power, and the fact that power can become unjust and tyrannical (*The Ecumenical Review*, July 1971, p. 247).

It is when the question of the *means* of exercising (or seeking) power is raised that we confront the question of violence. *How* can the present order of things be changed so that power is more equitably distributed? Can the change come about in a smooth, orderly fashion, or must it come in violent cataclysmic fashion? Thomas Melville, reflecting on several years as a Maryknoll priest in Guatemala, sees this clearly: "The question that is posed today is not yes or no to revolution, but rather revolution with or without violence." One of the most perceptive Latin American theologians, Professor José Miguez-Bonino, indicates the context in which the question of violence as a means of producing social change must be placed:

> An ethic of revolution cannot avoid discussion of the use and justification of violence. This question, nevertheless, needs to be placed in its proper perspective as a subordinate and relative question. It is *subordinate* because it has to do with the "cost" of desired change—the question of the legitimacy of revolution is not decided on the basis of the legitimacy of violence and vice versa. Violence is a cost that must be estimated and pondered in relation to a particular revolutionary situation. It is *relative* because in most revolutionary situations—at least those with which we are concerned—violence is already a fact constitutive of the situation. Injustice, slave-labor, hunger, exploitation are forms of violence that must be weighed against the cost of revolutionary violence (*The Development Apocalypse*, p. 108).

Many people counter such assertions by insisting that there is nothing new or unusual about this situation. Regrettable though it may be, there has always been injustice and there have always been abuses of power; no fundamental change is really possible. Such a response fails to take into account one very new factor, *the realization by the powerless that they need no longer remain powerless*, and that they can now

tional violence" is useful; an important breakthrough was achieved on the racial scene when whites began to see that they were guilty of "institutional racism"—that although individually they might be free of deeply ingrained "race prejudice," they were members of institutions in society that kept nonwhites in subordinate and demeaning positions socially, economically, and politically. "The violence of the status quo" is another way to describe the same basic phenomenon: *the way things now are* works violence against extraordinary numbers of those within our society.

Another useful distinction is that between "overt" and "covert" violence, the latter standing for the violence that is hidden within the life of society. The difficulty with this distinction, however, is that the so-called covert violence is not covert at all to those who are its victims, and it is thus an elitist term implying a violence hidden only to those fortunate enough to be on the uppermost rungs of the social scale.

In the present discussion we will use the term "structural violence," which is broad enough to embrace all of these implications. Some of the ramifications of structural violence are indicated in a recent publication of the ecumenical Commission on Society, Development and Peace:

> Violence can have structural forms built into the apparently peaceful operations of society as well as overt physical expressions. The failure to provide educational opportunity, or the manipulation of sources of information, can do violence to those affected. The existence in a society of intellectual repression in any form is psychological violence. The condescension and subtle forms of discrimination with which age sometimes treats youth or men treat women, or one race or religious group may treat another, are a part of it. We live in a society in which the drive for security, self-esteem or power, and the failure to share responsibility and decision-making often do violence to other persons. . . . Violence is therefore a condition of which all of us are guilty in some degree (*Peace —The Desperate Imperative*, pp. 13-14).

We must acknowledge, if we take this analysis seriously, that the structures of institutions of our society contain within themselves elements that *do* violate the personhood of many of those within the society. It is thus linguistically proper to speak, for example, about the violence of the slum—not the violence *in* the slum, but the violence *of* the slum. The difference between the two phrases is important. It is not enough to say that violent acts, such as mugging, rape, or robbery, take place *in* a slum environment. The point is that the slum environment, the structure of the slum itself, works violence against those who live within it, even if they never experience the physical harm so often attendant on slum dwelling. They are denied the possibility of achieving full personhood, since living in the slum means that they will probably not get the health care to which human beings are entitled; their children will almost surely go to inferior schools; because of inferior schooling, their children will almost certainly have to take inferior jobs; as a result, they too will have to live in inferior neighborhoods; *their* children, in turn, will most likely have to go to inferior schools—and the vicious cycle will be repeated in each generation. All of this adds up to "violation of personhood" and is a clear example of structural violence.

Other examples come to mind: Mexican-Americans in California quite properly feel that violence is being perpetrated against them when they are denied the possibility of bargaining collectively for decent wages, or legislation is introduced in Sacramento to deny them legal redress of their grievances. Workers in Latin America feel that violence is being done to them by American industries in their country that pay inadequate wages and then siphon off the immense profits for stockholders in the United States, rather than investing those profits to build an economy that will produce a greater measure of social justice. That, too, is structural violence.

These are the realities the Geneva Conference on Christians in the Technical and Social Revolutions of Our Time was describing in one of its reports:

> Violence is very much a reality of our world, both the overt use of force to oppress and the invisible violence (*violencia blanca*) perpetrated on people who by the millions have been and still are the victims of oppression and unjust social systems (Abrecht and Thomas, eds., *World Conference on Church and Society*, p. 115).

Let us sum up where the discussion has brought us. The structures of society in which we participate produce an inordinate and intolerable amount of suffering, destruction, and violation of human personality. This happens not just to a few of the human family but to the great majority. In a world in which two-thirds of the inhabitants go to bed hungry every night, we cannot pretend that violence is not being exercised against them. This is a world in which people like John F. Kennedy, Martin Luther King, George Wallace, and hundreds of thousands of Vietnamese peasants have been victims of direct physical violence; it is also a world in which our social structures condemn millions of black citizens to perennial despair, and in which the financial well-being of the white minority is in large part purchased at the expense of the dark-skinned majority.

Acknowledgment of the ongoing reality of indirect structural violence in society means that we must see violence (in the sense of "violation of personhood") being done not only (a) when a cop hits a kid or a kid hits a cop, and (b) when an American President orders the invasion of a neutral country in an attempt to salvage "national honor," but also (c) when a child dies of starvation in Guatemala because the dictatorial regime and American business interests conspire to deny the child's father a living wage, and (d) when a black child wastes away in an Oakland slum because the white power structure pays insufficient attention to providing better schools or job opportunities for the slum's inhabitants. Structural violence is the heart of the problem.

4. Structures That Benefit Us Often Work Violence Against Others

If we accept the truth that structural violence is the heart of the problem, and that the structures of our society do indeed work violence against many of its members, we still have not explored the full and disturbing implication of that truth, which is that those structures that benefit us most are frequently the ones that work the greatest violence against others. There are two issues here: one is the descriptive truth or falsity of the statement, while the other is the degree of moral responsibility the beneficiaries bear for the evil that is done to others by those same structures.

It is hard to gainsay the descriptive truth of the statement. White middle-class people, for example, benefit handsomely from police and judicial systems. Their suburban homes are protected from invasion by ghetto gangs in a way that ghetto apartments cannot possibly be protected. If a white person is arrested, he usually has access to good legal help and the means to pay for it. In a trial by jury, most of the jurors will be from backgrounds like his own, and the same language, customs, and *mores* will be shared. When a black is arrested, however, he may well be roughed up in the process, and he will usually not have the means to get expert legal help. The court will assign him a "public defender" who has no *necessary* interest in his case and no financial incentive to work hard for an acquittal. The jury may have no members who share the same background as the accused. It will be hard for him to get public attention focused on his case, particularly if he has no "connections." Overall, it will be notoriously more difficult for him to get justice than for his white counterpart.

Selective Service provides another example of inequity, even though it was presumably designed to avoid inequity. When draft calls were high a few years ago, twice as many blacks as whites proportionate to their numbers were called up and sent to Vietnam. The reasons are not hard to find: many whites got college deferments unavailable to blacks, since most of the latter had received inferior educations and could not get into college; whites who did not want to be drafted had financial resources to hire lawyers who could help them find legal loopholes for exemption; most whites knew about provisions for conscientious objection and many had the education to fill out the sophisticated forms with which uneducated blacks would have difficulty even if they learned that such an option was open to them; the personnel of draft boards who heard and passed on hardship cases were almost exclusively white. The structure that made it possible for most whites to get fair treatment almost always militated against blacks getting fair treatment.

Who is responsible? Is the inhabitant of suburbia to be held morally accountable for the special privileges of police protection he receives at the cost of neglect or repression in the ghetto? Is the white nineteen-year-old who escapes military service responsible for the death of the black nineteen-year-old who went to Vietnam in his place?

These are not easy questions and we will not presume to offer full answers. But it is hard to avoid the conclusion that those who enjoy the benefits of the structures, and are rendered comfortable and secure by them, are to that degree implicated in the violence to which those structures lead. This does not mean that such persons are engaging in direct physical violence against those whom the structures destroy: they may never have lifted a hand in anger against another person. But from the perspective of those who are systematically destroyed by structural violence, the beneficiaries must surely be held accountable.

Such an analysis often draws sharp rebuke from those who insist that we are morally accountable only for those things we individually and directly will. But the rebuke neglects the degree to which we are social and communal beings and not merely individual beings. To the degree that we are part of the evil our group is doing, and do nothing in the face of that evil, we share complicity.

A hard truth. But an important one. Perhaps in our era apathy is the unforgivable sin.

CHAPTER FOUR

Enter: The Voice of the Third World

*Our people see the social inequities, and they are coming to realize that
they need not live that way forever. . . . The choice is not between
the status quo and change; it is between violent change and
peaceful change.*

> The working draft of the Medellín Conference
> of the Latin American Episcopate, 1968

THROUGHOUT THE PRECEDING CHAPTERS there have been references to
voices from the "third world," with the clear implication that we have
much to learn from them. It is now time to listen more directly to those
voices to see how they can contribute to the argument we have been
advancing.

Why Turn to the Third World?

Before answering this question we must clarify a lingering misunder-
standing. "Third world" is a convenient (though sometimes misleading)
shorthand term that came into use at the Bandung Conference in 1955
to describe those nations not then committed to the "world" of capitalism or the "world" of communism, and thus comprising a "third world."

The nations so described include an extraordinary portion of the human family, living in Asia, Africa, and Latin America, and made up predominantly of those who are dark-skinned, exploited, and poor. Statistically the term third world is misleading, for as those who inhabit such countries point out, the proper term would really be "two-thirds world"—a fact that the white minority of the human family would do well to remember. The term is resented by many of those to whom it is applied, on the ground that no single term can appropriately describe the great variety of people who live in the third world. There is justice in the resentment. How, indeed, can Bolivian farmers, Indian scholars, and African tribesmen be lumped together in a single category?

In spite of these difficulties, however, we shall retain the term (until a better one comes along) as the most convenient way of describing that portion of the human family whose backgrounds and interests and concerns are so basically different from our own that we must listen to them carefully if we are not to remain hopelessly entrapped by our parochial class and nationalistic perspectives.

Why, then, turn to the third world to learn more about the reality of violence? First, because as is suggested above, American whites will have a distorted view of the world if we confine our perspective to our own portion, where it is relatively easy to be protected from the reality of continuing violence. Second, since whites are a minority of the human family, we need to listen to spokesmen for the nonwhite majority of the human family, most of whom live in third-world countries. While there are many nonwhite spokesmen in the United States, such spokesmen are increasingly articulate in their own right and resent being represented by white voices, whereas the voice of third-world peoples is not yet sufficiently heard in the United States. Third, and most important, Americans cause or support much of the misery and oppression in the third world, whether we are aware of it or not. We need, therefore, to learn about the extent of the structural violence we inflict, so that we can work to diminish it and obviate the need for violent revolt on the part of those who are deprived of power by our misuse of it.

The last point is worth elaboration. It is an uncomfortable but inescapable truth that much oppression of third-world peoples stems from American foreign policy and economic power, which work to their disadvantage. Even the most minimal acquaintance with the literature from South America, for example, underlines this point. John Bennett has summarized much of the evidence in terms compelling enough to deserve extended quotation:

> Americans need to learn about the full effect of our government's policy of training the personnel of Latin American

armies and police in methods of counter-insurgency warfare. They need to know about American agents training the police in such countries as Brazil and Uruguay when there is so much evidence of torture used by police against the government's critics. They need to know about the activities of the CIA against governments that are leftist or open to the left. Its scandalous operations in Guatemala and in connection with the Bay of Pigs are matters of record that should disturb us when we hear of its presence in other countries. How large a part did the CIA have in the recent rightist coup in Bolivia? Did it have any responsibility for the cold-blooded execution of Ché Guevara? What is its present role in Chile? We learned about the massive intervention of the CIA in Laos much too late.

It is beginning to dawn on us that we Americans—in the use of our power in the world—have created a monster that is out of control. This does not mean that those who are involved in its activities are themselves monstrous persons. However, they are now the instruments of this mighty destructive force— which no one planned as a whole but which has grown ever since World War II as a result of our obsessive anti-communism, the dynamism of American capitalism, and our confidence in American problem-solving and in our use of military power. The monster is guided by the tendency to judge all developments in Latin America with reference to their contribution to stability and to a climate favorable to American business. The attempt to strangle the Cuban revolution shows how far our government will go when it feels threatened by left-wing revolution in this area (*Christianity and Crisis*, April 1972, p. 67).

Thus we not only have some things to learn from what is going on in the third world, *we are involved* in what is going on there, whether we like it or not. The issues are painted more starkly there than they usually are at home, but they are ultimately the same issues and they involve us in the same way. We thus have an obligation to hear some of the things that citizens of the third world say to us.

A Breakthrough: The Medellín Conference of 1968

For centuries the Roman Catholic Church in Latin America sided with the tiny minority of landowners who were exploiting their workers and condemning generations of peasants to misery and hopelessness. Gradually, a change has been taking place—the result of the doors that Pope John opened, the forward strides of the Second Vatican Council, and the imaginative leadership of a few priests and bishops. Much of this culminated in a conference of the Latin American Episcopate held in Medellín, Colombia, in August 1968. A number of documents issued before, during, and after this conference indicate the degree to which the problem of religion and violence is being examined in new ways. To some readers the material may sound quite leftist; it should be remembered that the documents are not communist propaganda but examples of the thinking of an articulate group of highly trained Roman Catholic theologians. (The quotations that follow are from *Between Honesty and Hope*, material collected by the Peruvian Bishops' Commission for Social Action and published by Orbis Books in 1970.)

One of the documents, issued by more than nine hundred priests at Medellín, is called "Latin America: A Continent of Violence." In response to growing talk about "violence in Latin America" as though this were a recent phenomenon, the priests counter by asserting: *"For several centuries now, Latin America has been a continent of violence"* (italics in original). They then define what they mean:

> The violence we are talking about is the violence that a minority of privileged people has waged against the vast majority of deprived people. It is the violence of hunger, helplessness, and underdevelopment. It is the violence of persecution, oppression, and neglect. It is the violence of organized prostitution, of illegal but flourishing slavery, and of social, economic, and intellectual discrimination (p. 81).

This violence, they continue, is expressed in the fact that the average daily caloric intake for Latin Americans is around 1,500 to 2,000 calories per person, whereas the normal level for adequate human sustenance is between 2,800 and 3,000 calories. The economic deprivation is just as bad: the average per capita income in Latin America is about $300 a year. In addition, over 50 percent of the Latin American population is illiterate. In the light of these and other facts, the priests press the point home:

> We call all this "violence" because it is not the inevitable consequence of technically unsolvable problems, but the unjust result of a situation that is maintained deliberately. Each day it becomes more clear that the great problems of present-day Latin America are rooted mainly in the political, economic, and social systems that prevail in most Latin American coun-

tries. It is a system based on the profit motive as the sole standard for measuring economic progress, which was condemned by Paul VI in *Populorum Progressio* (p. 82).

In the face of this pervasive violence (which is similar to what we have previously described as structural violence) the priests describe the "new element" that has been taking shape in this vast panorama of poverty, misery, and injustice:

> It is the rapid and growing self-awareness of the exploited peoples, who see a real possibility for their own liberation. For many this liberation is impossible without a fundamental change in the socio-economic structures of our continent. More than a few feel that the time has already passed for accomplishing this by purely nonviolent means.
>
> Because the privileged few use their power of repression to block this process of liberation, many see the use of force as the only solution open to the people. This same conclusion is being reached by many militant Christians whose own lives faithfully reflect the light of the gospel. . . .
>
> [In the light of the gospel] one cannot condemn oppressed peoples when they feel obliged to use force for their own liberation; to do so would be to commit a new injustice. If such a condemnation were to issue from the Latin American church, it would seem to be once again the "opiate of the people," the servant of those who for centuries have practiced the violence of exploitation and oppression leading to hunger, ignorance, and poverty (p. 83).

Recognizing the need for deep-seated change, the priests then insist that the Church must be involved in the struggle and that the hierarchy itself must take sides. We have already noted that for hundreds of years the hierarchy did "take sides," but always with the wealthy landed aristocracy. Now, however, the bishops are importuned by their priests to shift their allegiance from the oppressors to the oppressed:

> It is part of the hierarchy's proper mission to denounce in prophetic terms the situation of injustice that makes such change necessary. Moreover, its failure to oppose the violence of the oppressors will indirectly provoke justifiable violence on the part of the oppressed (pp. 83-84).

Warning against "an idyllic picture of violence" while yet emphasizing "the right of any unjustly oppressed community to react, even violently, against its unjust oppressor," the priests conclude with four specific proposals:

1. In considering the problem of violence in Latin America, let us by all means avoid equating the *unjust violence* of the oppressors (who maintain this despicable system) with the *just violence* of the oppressed (who feel obliged to use it to achieve their liberation).

2. Let us clearly and forthrightly denounce the state of violence to which the powerful—be they individuals, groups, or nations—have subjected the people of this continent for centuries. Let us proclaim the right of the people to legitimate defense.

3. Let us forthrightly and firmly urge the Christians of this continent to opt for anything and everything that will contribute to the authentic liberation of the Latin American and to the establishment of a more just and fraternal society in collaboration with all men of goodwill.

4. Let us accord these Christians a broad margin of liberty in choosing the means they deem most suitable for obtaining liberation and building such a society (p. 84).

This is a highly charged document that does not mince words. Even more about the mood of the conference can be learned by quoting from the Summary of a Working Draft prepared for the participants of the conference. It has less measured prose, but indicates even more clearly the passionate fervor of the churchmen:

Our people see the social inequities, and they are coming to realize that they need not live that way forever. If necessary, they will even go so far as to use violent tactics to overcome the present state of affairs.

There is no doubt that a revolutionary spirit pervades much of the continent. People are calling for bold and thorough transformations that will radically reform existing institutions. We should not be surprised to hear talk of violence, because the aforementioned conditions themselves are acts of violence against human dignity and personal freedom. What should surprise us is the patience of our people, who for many years have put up with a state of affairs that could hardly be accepted by anyone who has a clear awareness of man's basic rights.

The lack of technological development, the pigheaded oligarchies, and the foreign-based system of capitalism block the road to necessary transformations. They actively oppose anything that is against their interests, and hence create a general situation of violence. The choice is not between the status quo and change; it is between violent change and peaceful change (p. 179).

The Medellín document on "Peace" is more tempered in its approach to violence than the materials we have quoted thus far. It recognizes that the quick route to violence may frequently (as the document says, quoting *Populorum Progressio*) "engender new injustices, introduce new inequities, and bring new disasters" (p. 208). But it, too, recognizes the ongoing reality of the injustice that is called "institutionalized violence," caused by the "structural failings in industrial and agricultural undertakings" (p. 206). Those who have power and wealth are reminded that, if they cling to their privileges and defend them by resort to violent means, "they will be responsible in the judgment of history for provoking 'the explosive revolts of desperation' " (p. 207).

The route that is proposed for those who wish to work for peace, particularly in the light of the above-mentioned realities, is a point of capital importance. Foreseeing that the root problem is injustice ("Violence No. 1," as Helder Camara points out), the document echoes the proposal of Pope Paul VI, "If you want peace, work for justice," a formula that in its own turn is reminiscent of the writings of Reinhold Niebuhr a quarter of a century earlier. The Medellín document puts it:

If the Christian believes in the capacity for peace to bring justice, the latter is an inescapable condition for peace (p. 206).

This is a healthy reminder to those who think simplistically of peace as no more than "the absence of war." Third-world inhabitants know that even when no war is being waged, their countries are far from peaceful: "[Justice] is an inescapable condition for peace." When injustice is rampant, there is no peace, even if the countryside appears placid. The close connection between the two is symbolized by the name of the pontifical commission set up after Vatican II to deal with peace. It was called the Commission on Justice and Peace. There can be peace only when the structures of society are dedicated to justice. Thus the routing out of injustice, a form of structural violence, is the "next step."

Colonialism: Internal and External, Old and New

Another area in which the Medellín document on peace helps us to see ourselves in a new light is in its trenchant discussion of "colonialism" as a pervasive example of structural violence. The term has understandably been a term of opprobrium in third-world countries for many years. Most of them were at one time colonies of European powers, although this kind of political colonialism has virtually disappeared today. But what the old-style political colonialism represented has not disappeared. Its widespread domination over the lives of colonists has been replaced by two equally devastating, if more subtle, forms of repression.

The first of these is called *internal colonialism*. Political power, once exercised from a distance of thousands of miles by leaders of other countries, is now exercised by a few national leaders within the country itself. A handful of such men can often gain extraordinary political, economic, and military power that is exercised despotically to their own advantage and the ruinous disadvantage of all the rest.

The second form of repression is called *external neocolonialism*. Although direct political and economic control of the country by outside interests has disappeared, the *indirect* control is just as great as before and in some ways even greater because it is less immediately discernible. Whereas the "old" colonialism was mainly political, the "neo" colonialism is mainly economic. The whim of a large world power can control the economic growth or survival of a small country through the loans, goods, and technical assistance it either makes available or does not make available, depending on the immediate advantage to itself. The terms of a loan from a large country to a small country may be so exorbitant that the latter pays back more *in interest* than it received in actual money for the loan itself. The profits that come out of the investments made by the rich country in the poor country tend to be drawn back to the rich country, so that the economy of the poor country is not materially bettered. There is often a high degree of collusion between the tiny group of political and military leaders in the poor country and the economic and political concerns of the rich country. Frequently "military aid" goes to poor nations for the purpose of keeping their military dictatorships in power so that they can oppose leftist uprisings. It is assumed that "the enemy of my enemy is my friend." (See, for example, the materials in Myrdal, *The Challenge of World Poverty*, Pantheon, 1970, appendix on "The Latin American Powder Keg," especially pages 472ff; and MacEoin, *Revolution Next Door*, Holt, Rinehart and Winston, 1971, especially Chapter Eight, "The Armed Forces.")

The attempted intervention of the International Telephone and Telegraph Company in Chile is only a single illustration of the point. In October of 1971, ITT offered the White House an eighteen-point plan to insure "that Allende does not get through the crucial next six months," proposing a special White House task force (assisted, of course, by the CIA) to mount an extensive campaign of economic warfare, subversion, and sabotage against Chile. The purpose was to cause such chaos and disintegration that the Chilean army would have every right to "step in and restore order," and incidentally put back in power a right-wing government. No wonder the *New York Times* called the plan one of "breathtaking arrogance."

"Internal colonialism" combined with "external neocolonialism" is a tough combination to beat, particularly when American interests lend their support. It is a powerful form of structural violence.

Camilo Torres: A Revolutionary Priest Opting for Violence

We can get a fuller picture of the dynamics at work in the third world by looking at two individual churchmen who basically agree in their analysis of the widespread reality of structural violence but disagree about the way to overcome it. The first of these is Camilo Torres. Torres, a Roman Catholic priest, grew up in an aristocratic and bourgeois family in Colombia. He was educated in Belgium at the University of Louvain, after which he returned to Bogotá as chaplain of the National University. Becoming more and more aware of the social injustice around him and of the unwillingness, or inability, of political groups to work for significant change, Torres sought to unite various leftist groups in a coalition that would have some power. His activities, creating many enemies within both state and church, were hampered more and more by the insistence of his religious superiors that a priest should stay out of politics. Finally Torres appealed for and was granted laicization. As his notoriety increased, his life was endangered, and friends urged him to flee to Louvain for more study in a safer atmosphere. Instead he chose to go to the mountains with a band of guerrilla forces to work for the overthrow of the oppressive government. Shortly thereafter he was killed by government forces in a guerrilla skirmish.

Torres said that he became a revolutionary as a Colombian, a sociologist, a Christian, and a priest. As a Colombian, he could not be a stranger to his people's battles; as a sociologist, he had certain skills of social analysis he could offer as a way of producing change; as a Christian, he believed that "the essence of Christianity is love of neighbor and only through the revolution can the welfare of the majority be attained"; and as a priest, he felt that surrender of himself to the needs of his neighbor was "a requisite of fraternal charity."

Torres saw clearly that individual charity would not be sufficient to change the old order. Since the violence was rooted in the structures, only structural change would be adequate:

> We do not serve our neighbor by giving him old shoes or left-overs from the table of the rich. We serve our neighbor with a fundamental agrarian reform, with free education, with the reasonable distribution of the riches, with equality of opportunity for everyone. And since these are accomplished only by taking power, then it is necessary to revolt in order to take power (Guzman, *Camilo Torres*, p. 78).

Torres did not feel that the transfer of power had to be accompanied by violence: "I am convinced that we must first try every peaceful means." He believed, however, that the final decision about the means of the transfer of power from the rich minority to the poor majority would not be made by guerrilla fighters but by the minority that was entrenched in power:

> It all depends on the way in which the oligarchy decides to forego its power. If it will choose a peaceful way, the people will assume power in a peaceful manner; but if the bourgeoisie does not want to surrender power, and chooses to struggle violently, then the people will respond with violence, because I believe that the people have a sufficient justification for a violent struggle (IDOC, *When All Else Fails*, p. 162).

Thus, if only violent means were left, violent means were justified.

The steps in Torres' move to violent revolution can be drawn from his "Message to Christians," issued shortly before his death. (1) The fundamental impulse comes from the gospel: "The essential thing in Catholicism is love toward one's neighbor." (2) Love must be embodied in the structures of society, and not be left to individual caprice: "I realized that in Colombia it was not possible to give effect to one's love for one's neighbor by simple beneficence, but that one had to change the economic, social, and political structure of the country." (3) The concern for the well-being of the neighbor must be translated into a practical program for change: "[If] everything that has been called 'charity' does not arrive at giving food to the greater part of the hungry, nor in dressing the majority of those who are naked . . . then we must seek effective means to ensure the well-being of this majority." (4) If those in power will not share it peaceably, the effective means of change will involve revolution: "It is therefore necessary to take power from the hands of the privileged minorities and give it to the majority of the poor. This, if it is done rapidly, is the essential of a revolution. The revolution may be peaceful if the minorities [refrain from] violent resistance. Revolution is therefore the way of obtaining a government that will give food to the hungry." (5) Convinced that all means of persuasion, discussion, moral exhortation, or political activity had been rendered fruitless in his own situation, Torres was left with no choice but to join the guerrilla forces in order to hasten the overthrow of the oppressive minority in power and thus root out the structural violence it was maintaining against the oppressed majority: "Revolution is not only permitted, but indeed becomes obligatory for Christians who see it as the only ample and effective means of realizing their love for humanity" (pp. 159-62).

Helder Camara: A Revolutionary Bishop
Opting for Nonviolence

Archbishop Helder Camara of Recife, Brazil, whom we have already encountered in our discussion of the "spiral of violence," agrees with Camilo Torres about the reality of "structural violence," which Dom Helder calls "Violence No. 1" or injustice. Convinced that no tinkering around the edges of structural change will suffice, he insists that deep-seated change is needed. He is thus a true "revolutionary," and is seen by the Brazilian government as such. He is now denied access to radio and television, and a number of attempts have been made upon his life. Several years ago he moved out of the large "episcopal palace" that was built for one of his predecessors, and he now lives in a single room in a small church in the poorest area of Recife. He has been involved in the creation of numerous "people's movements," and has encouraged his priests to participate in activities and structures that will increasingly challenge the legitimacy of the corrupt status quo. He says that he can honor the memory of Camilo Torres and Ché Guevara, who finally opted for violence, since they were concerned about injustice, as well as the memory of Martin Luther King, who was also concerned about injustice but worked in nonviolent fashion for its eradication. He then goes on to say:

> I accuse the real authors of violence; all those who, whether on the right or on the left, weaken justice and prevent peace. My personal vocation is that of the pilgrim of peace, following the example of Paul VI; personally I would prefer a thousand times to be killed than to kill (*Church and Colonialism*, p. 109).

Dom Helder offers two reasons for affirming nonviolence as the way of achieving the necessary revolution that will transform the structures of injustice. The first of these is simply an appeal to the gospel to which he as a Christian is committed:

> It is enough to turn to the beatitudes—the quintessence of the Christian message—to discover that the choice for Christians is clear: we Christians are on the side of nonviolence, which is by no means the choice of weakness or passivity. Nonviolence means believing more passionately in the force of truth, justice, and love than in the force of wars, murder, and hatred (pp. 109-10).

But hard on the heels of the appeal to the gospel is an appeal to realism of the most hardheaded sort:

> If this appears to be mere moralizing, be patient a moment. If the option for nonviolence has its roots in the gospel, it is also based on reality. You ask me to be realistic? Here is my answer: If an explosion of violence should occur anywhere in the world, and especially in Latin America, you may be sure that the great powers of the world would be immediately on the spot—even without a declaration of war—the super powers would arrive and we would have another Vietnam. You ask for more realism? Precisely because we have to achieve a structural revolution it is essential to plan in advance a "cultural revolution"—but in a new sense. For if mentalities do not undergo a radical change then structural reforms, reforms from the base, will remain at the theoretical stage, ineffective (p. 110).

How can those in other parts of the world "help" in a situation as desperate as that of Latin American countries? Dom Helder encourages them to work on the structural violence inherent in their own nations:

> To the youth of developed countries, both capitalist and socialist, I would say: instead of planning to go to the third world to try and arouse violence there, stay at home in order to help your rich countries discover that they too are in need of a cultural revolution which will produce a new hierarchy of values, a new world of vision, a global strategy of development, the revolution of mankind (p. 111).

Three ingredients will be needed in the overall task. Dom Helder's concern is that he and we become "fit instruments to perform the miracle of combining the violence of the prophets, the truth of Christ, the revolutionary spirit of the gospel—but without destroying love."

Such a combination is indeed, as he says, a miracle. Perhaps only such a miracle can save us.

Similar Diagnoses, Different Remedies

It would have to be acknowledged that a voice like Helder Camara's, urging nonviolence, is a minority voice on the South American scene. But between the two of them, Camilo Torres and Dom Helder represent the range of approaches that are increasingly emerging on the world religious scene. Both acknowledge the reality of structural violence as well as the need for a fundamental reorganization of the unjust structures. But there is still significant divergence over the legitimacy of overt violence in bringing about the needed reorganization.

This tension is mirrored in the report of the Geneva Conference of 1966 on Christians in the Technical and Social Revolutions of Our Time, the first ecumenical conference in which there was significant third world representation. One group of delegates reported:

> The question often emerges today whether the violence which sheds blood in planned revolution may be a lesser evil than the violence which, though bloodless, condemns whole populations to perennial despair. . . . It cannot be said that the only possible position for the Christian is one of absolute nonviolence. There are situations where Christians may become involved in violence. Whenever it is used, however, it must be seen as an "ultimate recourse" which is justified only in extreme situations (*World Conference on Church and Society*, pp. 115-16).

Another section of the conference, working independently, came to a similar conclusion:

> In cases where such changes [i.e., from unjust to more humane structures of human life] are needed, the use by Christians of revolutionary methods, by which is meant violent overthrow of an existing political order—cannot be excluded *a priori*. For in such cases it may very well be that the use of violent methods is the only recourse of those who wish to avoid prolongation of the vast covert violence which the existing order involves (p. 143).

We are approaching the crossroad at which we must ask the question, "Are there alternatives to violence?" But first we must consider how much we can extrapolate from the third-world situation to our own, and where the logic of the argument is leading us.

CHAPTER FIVE

An Interlude for Stock-Taking or, Where Is the Argument Leading Us?

What is so disturbing is not the appalling actions of the "bad" people but the appalling silence of the "good" people.
Martin Luther King, Jr.

A revolution is interesting insofar as it avoids like the plague the plague it promises to heal.
Daniel Berrigan, S.J.

THE ARGUMENT IS LEADING US IN uncomfortable directions, particularly if we take seriously, as we must, the right of the third world to a hearing.

Briefly summarized, the argument goes something like this:

1. Violence in our day is much more widespread than we like to admit. It is present not only in obvious overt physical acts of destructiveness like war, but also in more subtle forms of violation of personhood that characterize the structures of our society.

2. The victims of this structural violence are a majority of the human family. They are increasingly aware that their exploitation is morally outrageous, and they are searching for ways to change the structures.

3. Those who enjoy the advantages of the present structures are a minority of the human family. In spite of that fact, they have most of the power—political, economic, and military—and they have no intention of relinquishing it. Demands for social justice are a threat to their security and force them into a defensive posture, thereby polarizing society.

4. To the degree that justice is on the side of the exploited majority, we can be sure that pressures for fundamental change will continue to develop.

5. To the degree that change continues to be resisted by the exploiting minority, we can be sure that means for achieving change will move toward the employment of widespread physical violence.

6. The decision about whether such change comes peacefully or violently rests in large part with the minority in power: will they relinquish at least some of that power peacefully, or must it be taken from them violently?

7. The relinquishment of power will mean basically the creation of a more just society in which disparities between rich and poor will be narrowed if not eliminated, in which political power will not be in the hands of the few but shared among the many, and in which all individuals and groups can have a say in creating their own destinies, rather than being manipulated by the rest.

Point 7 is a minimal description of what might be true after the revolution—whether the revolution is violent or nonviolent, slow or fast, peaceful or warlike. And it is the bridging of the gap between point 6 and point 7 that seems so desperately hard to achieve.

Can There Be a "Just Revolution"?

Suppose the gap remains. Suppose those with power clutch it more aggressively than before, and the injustices that are the content of structural violence become increasingly worse. Is it legitimate in that case to use physical violence to overcome structural violence? Could there be, in other words, a "just revolution" analogous to a just war? Let us see how such an argument would be constructed.

In simplest terms, the case would be made that structural violence can become *so* deep-seated, *so* powerfully entrenched, and *so* destructive and despotic that there remains no way to overthrow it short of physical violence. The need to overthrow it by such means is not only permissible, but is *demanded* in the name of justice, equality, and love. To shrink from the use of violence on the relatively small scale of the quick overthrow of a despotic government is to give tacit approval to the continuing use of structural violence on a massive scale by that same government. As the Brazilian sociologist Jalles Costa puts it:

> I do not opt for violence, it is forced upon me. I have no other choice. If I opt for nonviolence I am the accomplice of oppression, I take sides on behalf of the violence of the state. . . . The Christian temptation is to have faith in a naive and ineffective nonviolence (*IDOC International*, May 1969, p. 64).

No one opting for this position will do so lightly, as the quotation itself makes clear. Nor is it morally permissible to urge the position on someone else while the urger remains detached at a safe distance; Helder Camara is properly scornful of what he calls the "arm chair Ché Guevaras" while Richard Hofstadter has similar disdain for the "sidewalk Sorels." Violence-at-a-distance assumes a romantic aura; there is no aura of romance for the one in its midst. Nevertheless, there could conceivably be times when those on the outside support those on the inside who have made their own decision to engage in a just revolution.

> The action of those in rebellion, as of those at war, must be subject to moral judgment, both as to means and as to object. Those who are themselves in comfort and security cannot urge armed rebellion on others who would thereby face death or life imprisonment. Nor can they preach patient endurance of a suffering they do not have to bear. *But there can be a just rebellion as well as a just war and we cannot sincerely withhold support from those who have decided to face the certain suffering involved in such liberation* (*Violence in South Africa: A Christian Assessment*, pp. 76-77).

Some further distinctions are usually made. Those advocating a just revolution usually distinguish between the violence they must use and the violence that is used against them, emphasizing not only the structural violence that has made their revolution necessary, but also the moral distinction between what Régis Debray calls the "violence that represses and the violence that liberates." Reubem Alves describes the same phenomena with the vocabulary of "violence" and "counterviolence."

> Violence is power that oppresses and makes man unfree. Counter-violence is power that breaks the rod which enslaves,

in order to make man free. Violence is power aimed at paralysis. Counter-violence is power aimed at making man free for experimentation (*A Theology of Human Hope*, p. 125).

White Christians who immediately characterize such distinctions as cases of special pleading need to be reminded how quickly Christians in the past have supported violence on their own behalf and condemned violence whenever it appeared likely to be used against their own vested interests. Arend van Leeuwen has pointed out this internal contradiction in the Christian approach to violence:

> The Christian ethos is . . . entangled in a painful dilemma. If the traditional justification of war as the ultimate means of external self-defense for the sovereign state has lost its validity, then the right and duty of the state to maintain, by violent means, its internal order against the threat of revolution is no less radically questioned. Looking back over history from our vantage point in the atomic age, it is amazing that the same Christian ethos which has willingly blessed the whole course of increasing violence from the Crusades to the atomic explosions over Hiroshima and Nagasaki has reacted so differently in the matter of internal violence. There it has condemned the unhesitatingly less pernicious use of violence and, as a matter of course, has sanctioned the defense of the Christian status quo against overthrow by revolution (*Development Through Revolution*, p. 282).

Roger Shinn rightly calls it hypocrisy when "Christians in positions of privilege endorse violence on behalf of a biased law and order, but invoke moral denunciation against violence that threatens unjust order" (*Christianity and Crisis*, July 10, 1972, p. 168).

Criteria for a Just Revolution

A doctrine of just revolution, however stated, would not urge an indiscriminate use of violence under almost any circumstances, but only a discriminate use of violence under certain circumstances. What might those circumstances be? In *Movement and Revolution* Richard Neuhaus suggests that the criteria used to define a just war can be employed to define a just revolution. Building on his discussion, we can ask: with what kinds of questions would the proponent of just revolution have to wrestle?

1. The first criterion of the just war is the most difficult to transpose

to the just revolution. How could one argue that a revolution is *declared by a legitimate authority*? One would normally argue that legitimate authority is being *challenged* by a revolution and that the only legitimacy a revolutionary group could claim would be the legitimacy it gained *de facto* if it were successful.

But the other side of the coin is that a revolutionary time is precisely the time when "normality" may mean oppression and repression. Could a legitimately elected government stray so far from its legal and moral mandate that a movement to replace it might actually claim greater legitimacy? (Hitler's rise to power is a case in point. He was legitimately elected. But a conspiracy to replace him several years later could have claimed greater legitimacy.) Several years ago a number of Americans signed what they described as "A Call to Resist Illegitimate Authority," claiming that the United States government was exceeding its legitimate rights by drafting young men to fight in Vietnam, and that such illegitimate action legitimated resistance to the government's orders. Does the opposite of illegitimacy constitute legitimacy? It is such questions as these that the first criterion raises.

2. The revolution must be carried out *with a right intention*. Matters are less murky here. The impetus to revolution usually arises out of a profound sense of moral outrage that injustice is being perpetrated on a wide scale. The initial intentions are likely to carry a high weight of moral fervor and to appeal to generous rather than base instincts, since (in the early part of a revolution at least) the odds are against the revolutionaries and considerable personal risk is involved.

It is when the revolutionaries begin to taste success, or gain power, that the intentions need to be held up again for special scrutiny. It is easy for vindictiveness and motives of revenge to begin to predominate toward those against whom battle has been waged. Revolutions can easily degenerate into the exchange of one form of tyranny for another. Ignazio Silone, an Italian author who went through the disillusionment of seeing the Italian communists lose their "right intention," explores in novel after novel the crucial question: "Why is it that after the revolution the persecuted always become the persecutors?"

It is in relation to this question that the Geneva Conference of 1966 pointed out the need to "remember the day after the revolution," the day when desire for revenge and retribution is highest. The *maintenance* of the right intention is one of the most difficult criteria to meet. Albert van den Heuvel, formerly on the staff of the World Council of Churches, has seen this point clearly:

> The Christian community even within violent revolutions will plead for things like no indiscriminate killing, and even for

compassion for those now deposed of their power. This makes the Christian doubly vulnerable in the revolutionary system; he will plead against it as long as possible. If he takes part in it, he will always ask for moderation and the reestablishment of law and order. This means he will never be a popular revolutionary. . . . (Denys Munby, ed., *World Development: Challenge to the Churches*, p. 189).

3. The revolution can be undertaken *only as a last resort*. Clearly, the estimates on this criterion will range across the entire spectrum, depending on who is doing the estimating. A government in power will always believe that a revolutionary *coup* aimed against it was premature and that the issues could still have been successfully negotiated, while the revolutionaries will insist that there was every reason to revolt long *before* the actual outburst took place. In the United States, for example, a black who has been the particular victim of injustice might insist that any revolution comes at least 300 years too late, while a middle-class white could hardly entertain the notion that there would be just cause for a revolution in America now or at any time within the foreseeable future. Camilo Torres insisted on being sure for himself that *all* peaceable means had been exhausted in Colombia before he took to the hills, and most of those who end up in the revolutionary camp have traveled a long road of gradual and often reluctant radicalization. Anyone who is not psychopathic would prefer change without violence to change with violence.

4. The revolution must be waged on the basis of *the principle of proportionality*. The good that is gained must far outweigh the evil that will be inflicted in gaining the good. Such an assessment is difficult to make in advance and even more difficult to maintain in the heat of the battle. How much temporary injustice along the way to victory is justifiable for the sake of the greater justice to be achieved in the future? May a substantial (or even unsubstantial) portion of the present generation be sacrificed for the sake of a better world for future generations? (It was reluctance to answer this question in the affirmative that made Albert Camus unwilling to become a revolutionary.) Can some concentrated violence now be justified in the hope of avoiding more extended violence later? Are there resources available to keep vindictiveness in check?

5. The revolution must have *a reasonable chance of success*. This may well be the most important—and most difficult—criterion to meet satisfactorily. Few things could be more immoral than urging others to engage in a "lost cause" that has no real chance of succeeding. This is

particularly true when the consequences of losing may be not only loss of life and property for the few but also loss of liberty for the many, since a repressive regime that is unsuccessfully challenged becomes more repressive in order to thwart potential future challenge. As we noted earlier, there can be a romantic *mystique* of violence that condemns others to terrible reprisals when ill-advised challenges are met by over-whelmingly superior power. What is demanded here is an extraordinarily responsible counting of the cost ahead of time.

6. The revolution must be waged *with all the moderation possible*. If the reasonable chance of success is difficult to ensure in advance, the principle of moderation is difficult to ensure in process. It is related, of course, to the principle of right intention. The problem of moderation will naturally be crucial in its application to the use of violence, which must be kept to a minimum and, as far as possible, be directed against objects rather than people. Many questions will be posed in relation to this criterion: Can torture to secure information ever be justified under the principle of moderation? Is there any way to avoid excesses of violence in desperate situations, especially when the revolution is going badly? Are there any guarantees that minimal moral constraints will not gradually (or quickly) be eroded away as the stakes of victory or defeat become more urgent? These are only a few of the issues that need to be raised by any who are disposed to move toward violent revolution out of concern for social justice.

Are we any closer to answering our question about the possibility of a just revolution? Not at least until we have considered one further factor.

On the Validity of Different Solutions
in Different Circumstances

At the first assembly of the World Council of Churches in 1948, delegates from Europe and North America were preparing a document condemning technology for its debilitating effect on the life of man. They were stopped by a comment from Bishop Rajah Manikam of India, who said, "Before you condemn technology, will you let us have it, please, in India for fifty years?"

The point is well taken not only in relation to technology but also in relation to violence. What is needed in one situation may not necessarily be needed in another. What may be appropriate at one time may be inappropriate at another. The spirit of nationalism, for instance, can be dangerous in a powerful and established country, if that country flouts its national pride at the expense of another nation. But the spirit of nationalism may be essential in the early life of a young and developing nation, as it tries to build unity and direction out of previously divisive sectional loyalties. Similarly, a violent revolution may have been appropriate in America in 1776 (though the historical revisionists are having second thoughts about that one), but this is no guarantee that it will be appropriate in 1976 (though some disenchanted youths have had second thoughts about that one, too). Once more, it might be true that an attempt at violent revolution in a certain small South American country today could advance the cause of social justice, but it is unlikely that an attempt at violent revolution in a certain large North American country today could advance anything but the cause of social repression.

All of which means that there is no simple answer to the question, "Can there be a just revolution?" Any answer will have to be prefaced with the words "It all depends . . . ," after which the circumstances of the dependency will need careful exploration: Who is proposing the revolution? How strong are the revolutionary forces in relation to the regime in power? Is there likely to be outside intervention? Have all other avenues of change been explored? Is there reasonable expectation that the situation after the revolution will increase rather than diminish the spread of justice?

On Not Extrapolating too Quickly from South to North

Having been informed by the plight of the dispossessed in South America, we must now determine how the lessons accumulated out of their experience apply, or do not apply, to our own experience.

1. There is a tendency, frequently noticeable in the rhetoric of student revolutionaries, to view economic, political, and military oppression in a small dictatorship; conclude (possibly rightly) that violence is justified there in the name of social justice; and then immediately extrapolate from that to the American situation, similarly described as one of economic, political, and military oppression; and conclude (probably wrongly) that violence is justified here also.

Some will immediately contest the latter parenthesis. Why should violence not be justified at home as well as abroad? The answer to the question will depend on the degree to which one believes that there are still genuine options short of violence that can produce necessary social change at home. The white American, not particularly inconvenienced by domestic structural violence, will not feel that the situation is crucial, and will therefore believe that many options short of violence are still available. But this is where the white American had better develop a special sensitivity, since there are many other Americans whose lives and children are being destroyed by structural violence, and who consequently feel not only that the situation is crucial, but that all options short of violence have long since been exhausted. Fr. Theodore Hesburgh, until recently the chairman of the U.S. Civil Rights Commission, has been saying for a number of years that we are progressively falling behind in implementing concern for racial justice and that the situation of minority groups in our country is getting proportionately worse. The white Americans' preference for nonviolence may not, in other words, genuinely measure the degree of despair and repression that minority groups experience.

2. The theme of *counting the cost* must be seen differently in the United States than in many third-world nations. In most of the world, the oppressed have the numbers, even though the minority has the power. In the United States, however, those who are clearly "oppressed" —economically, politically, and racially—are the minority, while power is in the hands of the majority. This argues for a different strategy for social change. A violent student or black uprising, for example, is not likely to bring new justice to students or blacks, but extraordinarily repressive measures against them. Speaking of student unrest several years ago, Governor Reagan of California in an unguarded moment commented, "If they want a blood bath, let's give them one right now." Even though he later retracted the comment, there was no doubt in his mind whose blood would be shed, just as there should be no doubt in anybody else's mind on whose side the guns, tanks, and numbers would be found in the event of such a confrontation.

An example of the wisdom of counting the cost before resorting to violence was demonstrated during the famous "May Day" weekend in the spring of 1970, when a tremendous influx of students and Black Panthers gathered in New Haven, where a Black Panther trial was about to begin. Many youthful white revolutionaries descended on the New Haven green prepared for a weekend of rock throwing and more serious violence, intending to bait the police into retaliatory action brutal enough to radicalize the less venturesome. What saved the weekend from escalating into ugly violence, however, was the discipline of the Black Panthers themselves, who realized that any violence in New Haven would rebound most unfavorably against the Black Panthers and other blacks living in New Haven, long after white revolutionaries had gone back to their Ivy League campuses elsewhere. Consequently, the Panthers infiltrated the crowd and maneuvered militant whites out of the area, charging them with being FBI agents bent on provoking trouble (which, in all probability, some of them were). Thus the 4,000 members of the National Guard who had been mobilized at the edge of the town remained at the edge of town, and another Kent State tragedy was avoided.

3. A too-ready espousal of violence needs to be further challenged not only in terms of what violence does to its victims, but also in terms of *what it does to those who employ it*. The violence of the oppressed (which may have a certain moral justification) easily becomes indistinguishable from the violence of the oppressor. Discriminations tend to become blunted, and what starts out as idealism easily becomes crass opportunism. As Arthur Gish puts it:

> Replacing the violence of the oppressor with the violence of the oppressed may bring some change, but is far too inadequate a change. To continue in the old forms of violence is not revolutionary. Violence always tends to be reactionary, no matter what objectives it may be used for. First of all it looks on people as objects. When one begins to rely on violence, he comes more and more to depend on it (escalation). Often it becomes romanticized. Its use causes other means to appear more and more ineffective and irrelevant. It is reactionary because the user becomes deluded into thinking that he is accomplishing much more than he really is. Finally, violence is undemocratic. Since it uses unprogressive means, its end will include these elements (*The New Left and Christian Radicalism*, p. 139).

Many forms of delusion are possible here. A plausible distinction, for example, can be made between violence against property and violence against people. Many morally impelled revolutionaries insist that the former is sometimes legitimate even though the latter never is—or at least only in extreme situations. The Berrigan brothers have argued this point with great effectiveness, without the qualifier. But those lacking the moral and spiritual discipline of the Berrigan brothers need to be aware that there is an extraordinarily slippery slope from violence against property to violence against persons, and that once one starts down the slope, it is increasingly difficult to distinguish between the two. For example, the Cambodian invasion in the spring of 1970 prompted riots at Stanford University. During this period, a fire broke out at the Center for Advanced Study in the Behavioral Sciences at about 3 A.M. It was a clear case of arson, and the timing indicated that it was likewise a clear case of violence against property and not against persons. But the blaze destroyed the lifetime research of a visiting scholar from India —all the notes he had brought with him to complete a project of twenty years' duration. Was this not an act of violence against the person as well? It would be hard to dispute the charge that the fine line between violence against property and violence against persons was trespassed in this case in a tragic and irretrievable manner.

Once such a distinction disappears, other moral discriminations disappear also. If it is possible to engage in a "little" violence against persons, such an act can be justified as an effort to stop much more violence against other persons elsewhere. To be sure, the war protester made a point when he said to the court, "Why are you so outraged that I dropped a rock on a policeman in Harlem, but are not in the least bit outraged that your government is dropping bombs on civilians in Hanoi?" But the difficulty with pushing this line of response too far is that gradually *any* violence short of dropping bombs on Hanoi can be justified in the attempt to stop the dropping of bombs on Hanoi.

It is here that Daniel Berrigan's comment to the violence-prone Weathermen (cited at the beginning of the chapter) assumes a crucial importance: "A revolution is interesting insofar as it avoids like the plague the plague it promises to heal." The great danger, then, in the revolution that embraces violence is that at the end of the day, those who had hoped to heal society will have been transformed into another instance of disease.

4. It seems clear that those without power will seek more and more vigorously to attain it and will feel justified in using whatever means are necessary for that attainment. We can predict that, if there is not *some* voluntary sharing of power and goods, a time will come when the power is forcefully taken away from those who have it now. Thus the great problem, perhaps the greatest problem of our time and surely the most important problem for white Americans, is this: *Can those with power be persuaded to relinquish any of that power voluntarily?*

There is little historical precedence for an affirmative answer to the question. Nations or large groups do not surrender power, since that would jeopardize their self-interest and make them vulnerable to the power of others. Individuals may occasionally rise to deeds of genuine selflessness, but collectively they seldom do. Here is the truth in Reinhold Niebuhr's contrast between "moral man and immoral society" (a contrast he later said would have been more accurately rendered as "moral man and terribly immoral society").

Frederick Douglass argued powerfully back in 1849:

> Power concedes nothing without a demand. It never did and it never will. Find out just what people will submit to, and you have found out the exact amount of injustice and wrong which will be imposed upon them; and these will continue till they are resisted with either words or blows, or with both. The

limits of tyrants are prescribed by the endurance of those they oppress. . . . Those who profess to favor freedom, and yet depreciate agitation, are men who want crops without ploughing the ground (*Violence in America*, p. 451).

And yet, unless ways can be found to persuade those with power to share it more equitably in the interests of justice, we can only assume that the outrage of the dispossessed will increase until it comes to the breaking point. There may be several rounds in the spiral of violence, but sooner or later the injustice will provoke a revolt of sufficient proportions so that repression cannot destroy it.

Any modicum of theological or political realism would suggest that nations as such are not going to act contrary to their own self-interest and that appeals to altruism will go unheard. Consequently, it may be an act of great moral responsibility to suggest to those with power that it is precisely *in their own self-interest* to share it, since if they do not it will sooner or later be taken from them. The alternative to a more just social order will not be the indefinite maintenance of an unjust status quo working to the advantage of the powerful, but an increasingly uneasy tension, building up a head of steam that will one day burst the bonds that more and more frantically try to contain it. Gunnar Myrdal sees the matter clearly:

> No upper class has ever stepped down voluntarily to equality with the lower class, and as a simple consequence of moral conviction given up their privileges and opened entrance to their monopolies. To be induced to do so, the rich and privileged must sense that demands are raised and forcefully pressed, and that power becomes assembled behind them. At that stage, moral ideals in the upper class are given their chance to play a supporting role (*Beyond the Welfare State*, p. 227).

It is not in the long-range self-interest of those with power to perpetuate structures of injustice that will one day destroy those who desperately seek to maintain them. It is therefore not softheaded sentimentalism but rather the most hardheaded kind of realism to insist that the way to avert physical violence in our society is to overcome structural violence. The matter is one of utmost urgency for those countries, like the United States, which have such inordinate power in relation to the rest of the world. So the argument keeps taking us to a realization that the place where change is needed is precisely the place where power is concentrated. The basic violence turns out once again to be injustice, embedded in the structures of a society that favors the few at the expense of the many. If those structures cannot be changed peaceably, we have no reason to expect that they will not be destroyed violently.

The World Council's Grants to Combat Racism: A Case Study

There will thus be two kinds of tasks for those who have power and yet want to bring about change. One of them will be to seek ways to persuade those with power to share it (a theme we will pursue in the next chapter); the other will be to help those without power to get it. This second task is extraordinarily difficult, for it will often smack of paternalism or manipulation, and those who are its beneficiaries may often need, for the sake of their own integrity, to disdain the helping hand that is offered to them. But attempts must be made.

It is possible to learn some lessons from certain attempts that have already been made. One of the most instructive of these is a recent decision of the World Council of Churches to make a series of grants to combat racism, surely one of the most blatant examples of structural violence. Having made statements for many years about the evils of racism, the World Council moved in 1970 into the area of action by allocating $200 thousand to projects and groups designed to combat racism in various parts of the world. The criteria for such allocations were the following:

- To support organizations that *combat* racism rather than welfare attempts to alleviate the effects of racism.
- To help strengthen the organizational capacity of racially oppressed peoples and to support organizations that align themselves with the victims of injustice.
- To give special attention to groups whose political involvement might preclude their receiving help from other sources.
- To concentrate on gifts that could have maximum effect and by means of which support might be elicited from other organizations.

A total of about twenty grants were made in such countries as Colombia, Japan, the Netherlands, and Australia, but the priority was placed on grants designed to alleviate social injustice in southern Africa, including Zimbabwe, Namibia, Mozambique, Angola, and Guinea-Bissau, as well as South Africa. It was a condition of the grants that they would be used as the grantees saw fit, with the proviso that they would *not* be used for arms or "military purposes, but for legal aid and social, educational, and medical work." The response to the grants was cataclysmic, particularly on the part of certain white South Africans. The World Council was accused by the South African government of trying to promote racial wars, and certain South African correspondents began to describe it as "Murder Incorporated." Particularly upset were certain South African white liberals who had been trying for years to work for gradual change. They felt betrayed, since it was inconceivable that other white South Africans could approve the grants.

Here, then, is a rather classic case study of the problem of producing racial change. Liberal whites still believe in working slowly to bring about change within the system, while many blacks have come to a total distrust of the system—a distrust even more pervasive than that of blacks in the United States—and believe that only by the raising of black consciousness and leadership will viable alternatives emerge.

In a remarkable "Open Letter to a Friend in South Africa," Albert Van den Heuvel, then a member of the staff of the World Council, tried to meet some of the objections. He pointed out that years ago the World Council urged white South African liberals to give blacks "a sign that their costly nonviolent protest would be backed by their white brethren." For many reasons, that sign was not given, and polarization increased as the South African government enacted increasingly repressive legislation against all nonwhite groups. It became clear that backing white liberals was not enough to change things and that support must be given directly to black groups themselves since "a (liberal) minority within a (white) minority should not be the only voice for a silenced majority" (IDOC, December 12, 1970, p. 17). In dealing with racism, wherever it is found, it is not enough merely to support those who would like to see oppressive policies changed. Support must be given also to the *victims* of racism so that they can develop resources to work directly for their own liberation. Thus in South Africa black groups must be supported, and "liberation movements" in countries farther north in Africa must be supported as well, or the support becomes tokenism and an implied blessing of the status quo.

Van den Heuvel then dealt with three criticisms of the program. First of all, as we have already seen, the World Council was accused of supporting terrorist organizations that wanted to change society by "violent" means. He responded by noting the irony involved in describing acts by blacks as "violence and terrorism" when similar acts engaged in by whites are called "law and order." To their credit, a significant number of white South African churchmen have made the same point to their own constituencies: South Africa is *already* a land of violence, of the structural violence built into a repressive political and economic system that engages systematically in the violation of personhood of almost 80 percent of its inhabitants. If there is to be talk of violence, let it center on the present structural violence being done by the white power structure; if that is changed, there will be no need for future physical violence by the victims of the present violence.

A second response to the World Council grants was to discredit their source by describing the World Council as a "communist-inspired" organization. This is a familiar tactic in the United States as well, and is frequently used by those who do not want the Church to get involved in politics and social issues. Van den Heuvel responded that the issue under discussion was racism rather than communism, and that those who allow racism to continue unchecked are the ones who truly support communism, since they create a situation so morally intolerable that communism becomes an appealing instrument of liberation.

A third response to the grants was to state flatly that the liberation movements and anti-apartheid organizations would not in fact use the money for "legal, social, educational and medical work" as they had promised, but would buy guns instead. Van den Heuvel simply replied that whenever money is given, certain promises are made by the recipients and that in this case there is no evidence to suggest that black organizations are less trustworthy than white liberal organizations that have received money in the past. Such a charge, leveled only at liberation movements, is implicitly a racist statement.

An overall defense of the grants appeared in the *London Times* over the names of Ernest Paine, one of the presidents of the World Council, and Pauline Webb, vice-chairman of the Central Committee:

> Clearly there may be differences of opinion as to whether this or that grant is wise. There are two kinds of violence in the world: violence exercised from above by those in power, and violence resorted to from below by those who see no other way of securing the redress of their grievances. . . . It is unlikely that those exercising repression from above will favor any kind of help being given to their opponents. The World Council of Churches, like mankind at large, has still not solved the issue of how much force is justifiable in any kind of particular situation. Those who approved or shared in resistance movements in Europe thirty years ago must clearly be careful in their reactions to the present decisions. Meantime, for the churches of the world, piety is not enough. The program to combat racism aims at helping forward efforts to secure basic human rights and to do so within certain decreed and well-defined guidelines (*IDOC*, December 12, 1970, p. 28).

Despite the furor that arose in 1970, the World Council in 1972 doubled the goal of the special fund out of which further grants will be made in the future. Surely the most important implications of the action for white Americans are that those who are themselves oppressed must be given the opportunity to help themselves and not merely stand by as the nonoppressed try (usually vainly) to "do things for them"; and that when the issue of violence is raised, it is crucial to push beyond fears of possible physical violence in the future to a recognition of actual structural violence in the present.

We now turn to a further examination of ways of getting at the injustice of actual structural violence.

Käthe Kollwitz

CHAPTER SIX

Are There Alternatives to Violence?

*Those who make peaceful revolution impossible will make
violent revolution inevitable.*

John F. Kennedy

*Neutrality in a social struggle between entrenched and advancing
social classes means alliance with the entrenched position. In
the social struggle we are either on the side of privilege or need.*

Reinhold Niebuhr, *Love and Justice*

IF WE CAN AGREE THAT THE BASIC PROBLEM is "structural violence"—
and that unjust structures must be changed, then the question that
emerges is a question of means: *How* can the structures be changed?
Can we get rid of structural violence without resort to physical violence,
or will physical violence be necessary to do the job adequately?

We will respond to this question on three levels. Assuming that the
gross imbalance in the allocation of the world's goods and power is a
basic reason for structural violence in the *global community*, we will
first examine some approaches to closing the gap between the very rich
and the very poor. Then, realizing that what we do about the injustices

of our own *national community* will affect the way we exercise our power over other nations, we will examine a spectrum of possibilities for social change. Finally, on the assumption that the *religious community* has special resources to offer, we will explore in a final chapter the possible contribution of the churches and synagogues to the relationship of religion and violence.

The Global Community: Beyond Paternalism, or From a Theology of Development to a Theology of Liberation

We indicated in an earlier chapter that ours is a revolutionary situation and that there are mounting tensions escalating toward widespread physical violence, since in relation to one another the rich are getting richer and the poor are getting poorer. This remained the descriptive reality even after a United Nations "Decade of Development" devoted serious effort to bridging that gap by urging rich nations to make resources available for the economic growth of poor nations.

The World Council of Churches and the Pontifical Commission on Justice and Peace have also given major attention to this problem through a jointly sponsored ecumenical agency, the Commission for Society Development and Peace (SODEPAX). SODEPAX has done much creative work in sensitizing the churches and governments of developed nations to the need to make resources available, through an international monetary pool, for the economic development of underdeveloped nations. Specific attempts have been made, since the 1966 Geneva Conference on Church and Society, to persuade governments in developed countries to pledge at least 1 percent of their gross national product annually for such use.

It would seem the most elemental act of human compassion, let alone Christian charity, to continue to seek ways to close the enormous gap between rich and poor, or at the very least to lessen its enormity. As long as a few people have most of the wealth, and have it at the expense of the broken lives of the rest of the people, we are in a morally intolerable situation of global structural violence that must somehow be overcome. Economic aid from rich to poor has seemed an obvious way to overcome it. It is clearly necessary, economically as well as morally, that more resources be made available to those presently lacking them. There has been considerable sophistication in the approaches employed, recognizing, for example, that unless there are drastic reductions in the amounts spent on armaments, developed nations will not provide sums of sufficient magnitude to underdeveloped nations to make much difference, and also recognizing that some sort of international agency for allocating available funds will be necessary so that economic aid does not become a new screen for "economic colonialism."

One would initially assume that the poor nations would be grateful for such resources as have been made available, and that they would see an increasing flow of money and goods in their direction as the quickest route to economic viability and self-determination. And yet the recipients of development aid are beginning not only to see it as "too little and too late," but also to wonder if even immensely increased contributions from rich to poor would make any significant difference in the overall relationship between them. The very rightness of the concept of economic development is being questioned as follows:

- The present system of economic aid maintains a paternalistic relationship between donors and recipients. Those who pay the piper always call the tune, and those with the resources finally determine how the recipients shall use them.
- When economic aid *is* given to needy countries, it tends to shore up the repressive and totalitarian regimes in those countries. Precisely those elements in a developing nation that most stand in the way of significant social justice are rewarded by economic aid from outside. Such aid is often accompanied by military aid, to ensure that "subversive" or left-wing elements in the country do not gain sufficient strength to challenge the corrupt regime in power.
- Trickle-down gifts from rich to poor do not fundamentally affect the imbalances now existing; they merely tinker around the edges of an economic system that is fundamentally unjust, without frontally attacking the system itself. Economic aid becomes a way of "buying off" what should be increasing moral outrage at a system that allows the few to profit so immensely at the expense of the many. Only a very thorough reordering of economic priorities will make a difference.

The cumulative impact of these and other arguments is that economic development (whether by intent or not) effectively prevents any substantial change in the existing disparities between wealth and poverty. All that can be expected are minimal changes that will leave the great majority of the human family still condemned to marginal and submarginal existence.

This means that among churchmen in third-world countries there is an increasing shift from a "theology of development" toward a "theology of liberation." Reporting on this shift, the French theologian René Laurentin comments:

The word "development" has been rapidly devalued as a result of abuse done in its name. Indeed, it becomes more and more obviously true that "development aid" or even "development funding" results in chaining the underdeveloped peoples to foreign economies and integrating them into alienating systems and situations (*Liberation, Development and Salvation*, p. vii).

The alternative, a "theology of liberation," is just beginning to emerge. We have seen preliminary indications of its emphasis in the excerpts cited from the Medellín Conference, and these can be supplemented from the writings of the Latin American Roman Catholic theologian, Gustavo Gutiérrez. After expressing his own disenchantment with a theology of development for failing to remedy the dependence of the poor on the rich, Fr. Gutiérrez speaks forthrightly about the consequences of the liberation of Latin America from the stranglehold of foreign aid.

All these studies lead us to conclude that Latin America cannot develop within the capitalistic system. Thus a true development for Latin America will occur only through liberation from the domination of capitalistic countries. This, of course, implies there will have to be a showdown with the national oligarchies. Latin America will never get out of its plight except by a profound transformation, a social revolution that will radically change the conditions it lives in at present (*Theology Digest*, Summer 1971, p. 143).

This concern is placed in the context of a full treatment of the Biblical theme of liberation, understood not only as man's liberation from the bondage of sin and from the course of history, but also as "the political liberation of oppressed peoples and social classes." It is instructive to note that the Biblical paradigm for liberation, the exodus story, is wrapped up in the theme of the liberation of the children of Israel from an oppressive political and economic Egyptian overlordship, and is not simply an account of a spiritual liberation.

Just as it was not possible for the Israelites to reform from within in Egypt, Fr. Gutiérrez feels it is no longer possible to follow such a route in Latin America:

Attempts to bring about changes within the existing order have proven futile. . . . Only a radical break from the status quo, a profound transformation of the private property system, access to power of the exploited class, and a social revolution that would break this dependence would allow for the change to a new society (*A Theology of Liberation*, pp. 26-27).

The degree to which such needed change is likely to result in Latin America through economic aid supplied by the United States can be measured by asking how realistic it is to assume that such a program would be funded by either American businessmen or an American Congress answerable to them.

It is, of course, Fr. Gutiérrez's concern that the Latin American Church take sides in this struggle and "abandon the field of lyrical pronouncements." The Church, he says, can make its message of love believable only by breaking with the present social order: "The mission of the Church is to make a total break with the unjust established order and make a forthright commitment to a new society." Fr. Gutiérrez insists, "Instead of talking about the Church and the poor, we must become a poor Church," taking sides with the dispossessed at whatever risk to institutional prestige or security. It will even be necessary for the Church to rethink the matter of accepting financial aid from churches in wealthy countries:

> Financial aid can be self-defeating in its witness to poverty, since it could break down the solidarity with the poor which is so necessary. Further, it could dull [the churches] into settling for reformist solutions and superficial social changes that in the long run will only prolong the misery and injustice (*Theology Digest*, Summer 1971, p. 147).

Thus, although it is clear that a theology of liberation may prove costly to Latin Americans in its initial stages, Fr. Gutiérrez makes it equally clear that the Church should be willing to pay as high a price as it seeks to demand of anyone else.

What the shift from a theology of development to a theology of liberation tells us is that underdeveloped nations increasingly do not want the kind of "help" from developed nations that keeps them trapped in a dependency role. From this perspective the most important thing a country like the United States can do for a third-world country is to leave it alone; but even that is unlikely, since the United States is probably already involved in the internal affairs of the country. Thus any proposal for political or economic isolationism on the part of the United States would be unrealistic even if it were desirable—which it is not.

White Americans should find ways to change the policies of their own nation, so that both the internal structural violence we perpetrate on our own minority groups and the external structural violence we visit on other nations' majority groups can be overcome. So interrelated has the human family become that what we actually do domestically has great effect on what we potentially do internationally. If we engage in structural violence at home, we will surely export structural violence abroad, and each will feed upon the other. In *Spiral of Violence* Dom Helder Camara underscores the lesson: "It is vital for the developed countries to come to understand that, without a change of structures at home, a change of structures in the underdeveloped countries is impossible" (pp. 73-74).

The National Community:
A Spectrum of Possibilities for Social Change

Once we are aware that one of our most important contributions to the overcoming of structural violence abroad is to take steps to overcome structural violence at home, we face the problem of discovering the means for doing so. Here we can explore four points along a spectrum of possibilities for social change:

1. Using existing structures to reform the system.
2. Employing nonviolent means to challenge the system.
3. Developing new structures to replace the system.
4. Engaging in violent struggle to overthrow the system.

These four means are not all mutually exclusive; the first three can be practiced within a framework of nonviolence, and only the fourth involves a commitment to violence. The third, which could be followed apart from the others or in concert with them, represents a somewhat different approach. The first, second, and fourth alternatives would presumably be employed in that order, each successive step being taken only after the ineffectiveness of the previous one had been demonstrated. All four are derived from a conviction that "the system" is in need of change, but they differ in their estimate of how extensive must be the changes sought, and how radical must be the means employed. We will assume, finally, that the purpose of the change is to dispel or at least minimize the injustices the system perpetrates through its structural violence.

1. Using Existing Structures to Reform the System

We have already seen that Latin American theologians of liberation reject the option of change within the system as no longer viable for them. This does not necessarily mean, however, that it is not viable for us. The degree of its attractiveness depends on how fully people believe that the system under which they live is inherently good (or at least not inherently evil) and how fully they believe that the shortcomings present within it can be overcome without radical social surgery challenging the system as a whole.

The estimate one makes of such possibilities depends not only on an objective reading of the evidence available, but also on how well or how badly the system has treated the estimator. Upper-middle-class whites seldom feel that the American system needs drastic overhauling, since they benefit handsomely from it, whereas blacks living in urban ghettos may see no possibility at all for the improvement of their lot unless the system is drastically overhauled. (Those who have four aces, it has been remarked, seldom ask for a new deal.)

Perhaps the most fundamental principle of the democratic process is that change from within *is* possible, and that the process is structured to provide means for bringing about that change. The process can respond creatively when pressures are exerted: public officials who act irresponsibly can be challenged by the electorate and new officials chosen to take their place; Congressmen, who must remain sensitive to the mood of their constituencies, can be forced to rethink positions the constituents deem unwise, if subjected to letters, telegrams, visitations, and threats of removal from office through exercise of the secret ballot; pressure groups can organize around a given issue (such as ecology or war protest) and exert significant influence through rallies, marches, and lobbies; the public conscience can sometimes be translated into legislation that guarantees new rights to groups previously denied them, whether the issue be civil rights legislation, antipollution laws, or new provisions for conscientious objection.

Those who decry the extent to which laws *do* advance human welfare should ponder the words of Martin Luther King, Jr.: "The law can't make the white man love me, but the law can keep the white man from lynching me—and I think that's pretty important." Those who feel that laws by themselves are enough to advance human welfare should ponder the fact that, while the law could keep the white man from lynching Martin Luther King, the law could not keep a white man from shooting him.

There is clearly much that can be done within the system. With persistent political pressure, changes for the better can be effected, although pressures must continually be exerted not only to preserve gains already made, but to push in the direction of new gains. Although the effort expended often seems inordinately disproportionate to the minimal returns achieved, and the style of political engagement often seems plodding and unspectacular, the reason the system works as well as it occasionally does is because people do insist that politicians be accountable for their policies, harass them when they try to duck away from responsibility, and remind them that they are accountable on election day with their very jobs.

Those who give up on the system often do so prematurely after brief election-week forays of unproductive precinct walking, and quite superficially reject possibilities they have never genuinely explored. (One is reminded of the fifteen-year-old youth who explained his new addiction to Zen to Mort Sahl: "The gods of the west have failed me.") This is not to deny that there is tremendous disillusionment with the system, particularly among those under thirty who through their mature years have seen the system prosecute a dirty war in Vietnam and exploit minority groups at home. They need to be reminded that it is by bringing pressures to bear upon the system that it can—perhaps—be persuaded to avoid dirty wars in the future and start once again to become concerned about minority groups.

2. Employing Nonviolent Means to Challenge the System

It is the "perhaps" in the sentence above that persuades some people that it is not enough to work for political candidates, join Common Cause, attend precinct meetings, and needle Congressmen. They come to feel that too little is accomplished and that the structural violence in the system remains pervasive and insufficiently challenged. They reiterate the question raised by the World Council of Churches in *Study Encounter*:

> If the first option is chosen exclusively, is the tenacity and depth of structural violence taken seriously enough? Are there not groups in society permanently excluded from voice and influence thereby? Does not an apparently democratic justice in fact favor the rich and powerful? Can justice be achieved in a sinful world without real social dislocation of the powers that be? (p. 6).

While such persons may continue a measure of activity within the political process, they up the ante by significant challenge to the system through nonviolent protest. The point that needs stressing is that nonviolence is not (as it is frequently caricatured) a way of avoiding conflict, but a particular technique and positive force for *dealing with* conflict. It requires a level of discipline and courage that can endure the possibility of pain and defeat because the ultimate stakes are so important. It proceeds not only from a negative conviction that violence may be morally evil and tactically counter-productive, but from a positive conviction that nonviolence can be both morally correct and pragmatically effective in the long run if not always in the short run. Thus it is not correct to speak of nonviolence as an alternative to revolution but of nonviolence as a means of bringing about true revolution.

Andrew Young, who worked closely with Martin Luther King for many years, and who knows all about the setbacks and reverses of the civil rights movement in the early '60s, could nevertheless state at a World Council symposium in the early '70s:

> It is not popular these days to speak of nonviolence, but the record shows that it works. Whereas it was common a decade ago for black people to be shot for attempting to vote, they are now voting in increasing numbers and producing the transition from moral to political power we have dreamed and preached about. The challenge to the churches in the seventies is to achieve revolutionary change nonviolently.

As this book is being prepared for publication, Mr. Young has just been elected to the House of Representatives as the first black Congressman from Georgia in over one hundred years. He is now in a key position to help in the transition "from moral to political power."

The strategy of nonviolence can be communicated by recalling the six points Martin Luther King described in *Stride Toward Freedom* as pivotal for an understanding of the position:

1. Nonviolence is for the strong rather than the weak. It is a difficult discipline that eschews cowardice. It is not nonresistance but a particular method of resistance.

2. Nonviolence does not seek to "defeat or humiliate" the opponent, but to win him over. It is not employed for the purpose of scoring points but as a means of creating "the beloved community."

3. Nonviolence directs itself "against the forces of evil rather than against persons who happen to be doing evil." One may despise a particular form of evil, but one may not despise the doer of the evil.

4. Without making suffering into something to be sought, nonviolence can bring home the truth that "unearned suffering is redemptive." It can be creatively enacted in ways that transform evil into a potential for good.

5. The attitude of nonviolence must be within the heart of the individual as well as in his outer actions. "The nonviolent resister not only refuses to shoot his opponent but he also refuses to hate him."

6. Nonviolence "is based on the conviction that the universe is on the side of justice." The practitioner can believe that he is not going

against the grain of what is ultimate, but seeks rather to exemplify what is ultimate: redemptive suffering love.

Of particular importance in our discussion is the dimension of nonviolence that moves into civil disobedience. This tactic is generally misunderstood by those who do not practice it (and occasionally by those who do). It is important to see that it can be a significant catalyst for social change.

Practitioners of nonviolent civil disobedience are usually selective. They begin by accepting a framework of law as essential for the health of a society. Within the overall framework of generally accepted law, there may be a given law that appears manifestly unjust and perhaps even (in relation to the total body of law) illegal—a law that works a particular hardship on members of minority groups (denying them access to certain schools, housing areas, restaurants, and so forth). The law, in other words, is a clear example of the structural violence we have been examining in the earlier pages of this book. Efforts to change the law by means of pressure on lawmakers, meetings to sway public opinion, or use of the franchise prove unsuccessful. Subsequently a group of persons decides to focus attention more pointedly on the wrongness of the law by publicly and nonviolently breaking it, sitting in at a restaurant, for example, and refusing to leave when ordered in the name of the law to do so.

There can be two creative consequences of such an action: first, public opinion may be raised to a new level of consciousness by the more dramatic challenge to the law that civil disobedience entails, and others persuaded of its wrongness may help to get the law removed from the statute books; second, as a result of the arrest and trial that follow an act of civil disobedience, the constitutionality of the law can be challenged in the courts, and the local ordinance under attack may be found to be at variance with state or federal law and declared unconstitutional. (This in fact has been the result of cases similar to the one used in our hypothetical example.) There are thus many situations in which the reality of structural violence can be challenged by means of nonviolent civil disobedience.

Even if the given instance of structural violence is not immediately overcome, an act of civil disobedience can often have a profound effect on the collective conscience of those who are forced to ponder its implications. Perhaps the clearest recent example of this was the act of a group of Roman Catholic priests, nuns, and lay people, including Daniel and Philip Berrigan, who dropped napalm on draft board records at Catonsville, Maryland, to register their moral protest against American fliers dropping napalm on Vietnamese villagers. After the deed, they waited for arrest, stood trial, and served extended prison sentences. It was their belief that such a deed communicated, much more powerfully than words, something of the grotesque reversal of moral priorities that has taken place in America when men are imprisoned for dropping napalm on pieces of paper but are given medals for dropping napalm on human flesh. For many people, the juxtaposing of those two incidents of the use of napalm triggered significant reappraisals of the whole matter of American presence in Vietnam and potential American presence in future Vietnams.

The efficacy of nonviolent civil disobedience, then, rests on a number of factors. If the issue is chosen carefully, if the action is of a sort that communicates clearly, and if the participants indicate the depth of their commitment by the risk of personal jeopardy, such actions may be among the most important ways of challenging the structural violence of the system.

A final comment on the tactic: it may be that in the 1970s nonviolent civil disobedience should be particularly a white middle-class tactic. Blacks, Chicanos, and members of other minority groups have a notoriously difficult time getting justice in American courts and are often the victims of ugly discrimination in American prisons. Whites, who can usually afford lawyers and probably draw a certain degree of public attention to their actions, can more urgently be asked to consider such tactics when other alternatives have been exhausted.

3. Developing New Structures to Replace the System

Even when there are noticeable improvements in the system because of intense political activism and nonviolent pressures for change, the rate of change is painfully slow. Sometimes the movement seems to go backward. (The announcement by Mr. Nixon just after his reelection in 1972 that he was going to send "civilian advisors" to assist the South Vietnamese has an almost Kafkaesque quality about it, since it was President Eisenhower's decision almost twenty years ago to do exactly the same thing that started the American misadventure in Southeast Asia.) In addition, working within the system, to the degree that the positions just described demand, often seems to involve an almost total sellout to the system. To strain out one evil gnat involves swallowing a dozen evil camels. Furthermore, the ability of the system to absorb and neutralize enormous amounts of dissent without fundamentally changing leads certain people today to embody a counter-culture stance. They see the system as too powerful to destroy and too evil to accept, and as a result of repudiating the idea of reform-from-within, they decide that they will seek to embody *now* the kind of life that others assert is only possible in the distant future, after a great deal of reform-from-within or even "after the revolution." Just as a movie preview tells us enough about the coming attraction so that we want to be present for the full-length feature, so the adoption of the counter-culture stance tries to embody a preview of coming attractions by beginning *now* to live out some alternate life styles. Even though the new styles are not present in full force, they are visible enough so that others can see what the full-fledged experience would be like and perhaps be persuaded to adopt it themselves.

Instead of battering against the existing structures, in other words, advocates of the counter-culture decide to ignore the existing structures as much as possible and create new ones to replace them. In a world that seems increasingly insane and lacking in meaning, they will set up little islands of sanity and meaning; in a culture that is built on competition, they will seek to live in terms of cooperation; in a time when family loyalties seem to divide people, they will extend living arrangements to bind a number of families closer together; in a time when the rewards of regular jobs are frenetic fuss and ulcers, they will seek other kinds of employment that are fulfilling rather than debilitating. In Thoreau's over-used and under-practiced phrase, they "march to the beat of a different drummer." What is the point of winning the rat race if one is still a rat? The counter-culture position represents, in other words, a radical challenge to the values that constitute successful middle-class American existence—which may be why successful middle-class Americans seem so threatened by it.

To the degree that such a position can survive, it obviously offers a great hope for bypassing much of the structural violence of the present system and providing alternate structures that can minimize and increasingly replace that violence. Furthermore, this particular stance can be partially combined with others. One could adopt a counter-culture base, for example, and still be involved selectively in certain aspects of the political process, zeroing in on such issues as environmental control or fair housing or antiwar activity. It can be argued that this might create a *more* effective political presence than political engagement on a multiplicity of issues. Without some such measure of engagement in the wider society on behalf of others, in fact, the counter-culture movement could become élitist and ingrown, dealing only with the concern of a tiny group and ignoring widespread misery that demands short-term alleviation as well as long-term amelioration. But in concert with other strategies, it could offer a modest sign of hope in the midst of human bewilderment.

4. Engaging in Violent Struggle to Overthrow the System

Only after a significant attempt to embody the above positions does one have the moral right to weigh the option of physical violence as the "only way left" to bring about needed change.

One could weigh the option of violence and reject it, as entailing too great a cost in human life and suffering, and return to one of the other options with a greater sense of dedication, realizing in a new way how high the stakes are and how frightening is the alternative if one of the other options cannot be made to work. This has been the path followed by most of the practitioners of nonviolent change in our day. Martin Luther King, César Chávez, Helder Camara, the Berrigans, and others have confronted the possibility that the nonviolent revolution might need to escalate to a violent revolution, and they have returned to the nonviolent struggle more determinedly than before.

One could also weigh the option of violence and affirm it, however reluctantly, feeling that there is a greater cost in human life and suffering if structural violence continues unchecked than if one engages in certain controlled acts of violence to destroy those structures.

Much of the present book has been devoted to examining this position, trying to measure for "white Americans" the appeal it has for the nonwhite Americans and non-Americans who live in desperation. There is no need to rehearse those arguments again. There is need only to remind the white Americans to whom this book is addressed that the logic of this fourth position will appear more and more unassailable to a majority of the human family if those who disavow it or are frightened by it do not bend their efforts with extraordinary energy to ensuring that fundamental change comes by one or another of the *other* options we have examined. Let us face once more the theme of so much third-world literature: Change there will be; it is those with the power who will determine whether change comes violently or nonviolently.

So to our initial question, "Are there alternatives to violence?" the answer is "Yes." To the subsequent question, "Can we avail ourselves of those alternatives to violence?" the answer is, "If we do not, we will thereby contribute to the necessity of the violent alternative." Or, to cite again the epigram of John F. Kennedy, which is the description of our age and possibly its epitaph: "Those who make peaceful revolution impossible will make violent revolution inevitable."

Toward a Position:
"Selective Conscientious Objection" to Violence

We have examined a variety of positions on the relationship of religion and violence, from those that rule out violence as *a priori* immoral and unacceptable to those that are ready to invoke violence as a necessary and morally defensible vehicle of change. There would be something satisfying about being absolutely clear in one's own mind—and heart—either that violence was *never* permissible or that it was *frequently* permissible. But the complexities of decision-making about violence simply do not permit such easy choices. Furthermore, to elevate either violence or nonviolence into an absolute principle, and make all decisions in such a light, would be to forget that the issue of violence vs. nonviolence has to do with *means* rather than ends. Finally, we have also discovered that there is no simple way to extrapolate a specific ethical "answer" from one situation to a very different situation (from the actions of Camilo Torres in the mountains of Colombia to the actions of a war protester in the District of Columbia, or vice versa).

An alternative position on the relationship of religion and violence can be formulated by drawing both upon our earlier examination of the just war theory and upon the experience of many young men who were ordered to report for induction into military service during the war in Vietnam.

An individual who was not an absolute pacifist could not claim to be a "conscientious objector" in the only sense that the law presently allows. Yet many young men, who indicated that they might have been willing to participate in a war they considered just, refused to enter military service during the Vietnam war on the grounds that it was an unjust and immoral war and that they could not in good conscience participate in it. They reached this conclusion by examining criteria for a just war and denying the applicability of those criteria to the particular war that was then in progress. Such a refusal to serve put them in the position of being "selective conscientious objectors."

Because the position is not honored by law, individuals who persist in this conviction are sentenced to jail for refusing to serve in the Army. It should be noted that although the position is not honored by law, it is eminently honorable; virtually all the major religious bodies—Catholic, Protestant, and Jewish—have affirmed its integrity and have urged that provision for its integrity be written into the law.

This position of selective conscientious objection to war is a useful analogue to a position we could describe as selective conscientious objection to violence. One who cannot take a position that violence under every conceivable condition is absolutely wrong, who cannot be a conscientious objector to *all* expressions of violence, must nevertheless cope with the likelihood that under many and probably *most* situations it will be wrong. The moral obligation of the holder of such a position will be to develop his own criteria (perhaps similar to those described in relation to the possibility of a just revolution) and adhere to them rigorously.

Those who are skeptical of the viability of such an attempt will no doubt feel that when the existential crunch comes, the individual's resolve will falter, and he will find ways to rationalize whatever degree of violence seems expedient. But I believe there are possibilities of avoiding this conclusion, particularly if we remember from our earlier discussion that the initial presumption will always be *against* the use of violence. What will have to be demonstrated with overwhelming certainty will not be that violence can be repudiated but that it can be employed. The use of violence will always remain the exception rather than the rule.

My own anticipation is that the employment of such a moral calculus will almost always preclude the use of violence. There would seem to be no possibility of justifying participation in war in the atomic era, for example, and the unlikelihood of justifying violence in other arenas of human life today (save in certain extreme situations when all else fails) seems almost as certain. The position would appear to come very close, therefore, to a practical commitment to nonviolence as the most viable way to bring about needed change.

Why not, then, simply take the plunge and affirm the nonviolent position unambiguously? Two things make it impossible for me, at least, to go that route:

1. There is always a danger that those in relatively comfortable circumstances will remain naïvely insensitive to instances of evil that might demand more vigorous opposition than relatively comfortable circumstances would suggest. If (as I have been arguing) such persons should not extrapolate too simplistically from third-world situations to their own, neither (as I am now arguing) should they seek to impose their own solutions too simplistically on those for whom such solutions may seem irrelevant moral luxuries. I am not entitled to make a decision for my brother in the third world, though I will certainly listen to him in making my own decision in my own world, and hope that as he makes his decision he will likewise listen to me. But neither of us can place a binding commitment on the other.

2. It is necessary in reaching a moral position to allow, in principle at least, for the extreme instance, the *ultima ratio*, in which what would otherwise be ruled out might become a significant moral option. The obvious example is the decision made by Dietrich Bonhoeffer when he became a member of the resistance movement in Germany—a decision that meant a willingness to participate in the plot against Hitler's life.

Bonhoeffer underwent great anguish before he agreed to condone and take part in an act of murder. He would never have argued that the decision set a precedent justifying future murders. It remained for him the extreme instance, the exception from which it was not possible to argue to other possible exceptions. (Although he is close to Bonhoeffer in many ways, Daniel Berrigan has stated that it would *not* have been possible for him to participate in tyrannicide.)

We are left, then, with a position that must in principle allow for the possibility of violence as a last resort, when all else fails, but that will have numerous safeguards built into it to ensure that no one easily or prematurely decides that the last resort has been reached. If properly understood, this need not be a moral cop-out, either in the direction of allowing easy rationalizations for the use of violence, or in the direction of misinterpreting nonviolence as disengagement from conflict.

Those who hold this position will not seek suffering, but will be willing to risk it if necessary. And because the position is not negative, they will seek to act positively and directly within a framework that embodies "a more excellent way."

CHAPTER SEVEN

The Religious Community: Resources and Roles

Did not your father eat and drink
and do justice and righteousness?
Then it was well with him.
He judged the cause of the poor and needy;
then it was well.
Is this not to know me?
says the Lord.

Jeremiah 22:15-16, emphasis added

Any claim to non-involvement in politics . . . is nothing
but a subterfuge to keep things as they are.
Gustavo Gutiérrez, *A Theology of Liberation*

An impossible dilemma seems to confront white Americans:

We have great power—and we are told that we must share it or have it taken from us. We have great wealth—and we are told that it is immoral to be so rich while others are so poor. We claim that violence is abhorrent to us—and we are accused of perpetuating the very thing we disavow. We want to help people—and we are told that our "help" is only a disguised method of increasing our control over them.

What seems impossible is to move from one side of the paradoxes to the other. Who, having power, can bear to give it up? Who, having wealth, can handle a perpetually guilty conscience? Who, claiming virtue, can withstand the charge of hypocrisy? Who, desiring to help, can believe his desire is merely self-serving? And yet . . . suppose the charges are correct? Suppose we *do* practice the structural violence that is implicit in all the charges? Can we really change?

A Place to Stand

It is hard to see how we can face the depth of the change that is called for without a broader perspective than we usually have. The basis on which we are called upon to think and act must be wider than our class interests, our racial interests, and even (hardest of all for Americans) our national interests. And if the most inclusive term by which we can describe ourselves is "white middle-class Americans," such a definition is too partial and too parochial to enable us to find significant ways of transcending it in more inclusive terms.

Here, surely, is where membership in the religious community offers the possibility of a self-definition that is *not* partial and parochial. Whether we define our religious community in Jewish or Christian terms, the one thing of which we can initially be sure is that such a community is *not* exhaustively defined by such terms as "white," "middle-class," or "American." Both the Christian and Jewish communities transcend such terms and offer an all-embracing perspective that can give us a better and more critical view of ourselves. To describe oneself as a Jew or a Christian is to acknowledge community with many who are not white, who are not middle-class, and who are not American. It is to claim membership in a community where those characteristics are incidental and finally unimportant. It is to acknowledge a higher bond drawing people together—to recognize, for example, that *all* persons are made in God's image, that he is the God of Egypt as well as Israel, of North Vietnam as well as North America.

Perhaps from this perspective people *can* engage in acts that seem to threaten their security as Americans, if it turns out that they operate from a higher security than simply being Americans. There would be no reason to expect persons who are only or totally Americans to act in ways that could threaten their "American-ness" at all. But if their self-definition involves a further dimension—Jew or Christian (or Buddhist or Moslem for that matter)—they have a place to stand where critique and change are possible.

Communities of Creative Dissent

A place to stand, then, offers the possibility of a fresh perspective. And it is just such a fresh perspective that can enable those who hold it to challenge many of the things they would otherwise hold most dear. The God of Judaism and Christianity, for example, is God of *all* the nations: he does not love Americans more than North Vietnamese, nor is he more at home in Washington than in Moscow. In the name of such a God, flagrant injustice would have to be called flagrant injustice, not only when committed by Vietcong guerrillas but also when committed by American bomber pilots. Such a God would elicit a higher loyalty than loyalty to nation, race, or class. And such loyalty would make possible the kind of critique of *one's own* nation, race, or class that would otherwise seem impossible. To say "yes" to such a God would mean saying "no" to other gods and thereby making a definitive choice. Examples:

- Jews learned early that Jahweh's demands were exclusive: "You shall have no other gods before me." The Canaanite Baals could no longer be worshipped; neither could injustice be practiced without incurring the disfavor of the God who demanded justice from those who claimed to be his children.
- Christians learned early that to say "Christ is Lord" was also to make an exclusive claim; it meant refusing to say "The state is Lord," which is what the first-century state demanded of all its citizens.
- Thomas More learned later that the only possible answer he could give to the question, "Are you not the King's good servant?" was, "I am, Sire, the King's good servant, but I am God's good servant first." It cost him his head.

In each case, affirming God meant denying the claim of some other who wanted to play the part of God. The ability to dissent, to say "no" even to the claims of nation, race, or class, is the *sine qua non* for the development of a world in which structural violence is overcome. For when we cannot dissent from many of the demands that the structures make upon us, we become their captives and perpetuate their injustice in our lives. Fr. Régamey, a French Roman Catholic priest, has indicated that in the face of "the established disorder" of our times, "the most radical and urgent task of our time is to prepare men for eventual refusals to obey" (*Nonviolence and the Christian Conscience*, p. 255).

If what may be called for is "eventual refusals to obey," we may even need a stronger term than "creative dissent" to indicate what will be asked of us. Fals Borda, a Colombian sociologist, has begun describing the Church as "the subverting community." To subvert is "to turn from beneath"; it means not only refusing to give uncritical allegiance to the status quo and challenging the unjust structures of the society, but seeking for ways to move society in new directions. The word "subversive" has sinister connotations in the white middle-class American lexicon, but this is only because any suggestion of change is threatening to those whose security is challenged by the suggestion. In the basic meaning of the word, Jeremiah was a subverter; so was Jesus of Nazareth, who was put to death by the state on the charge of high treason. And any religious community in our day that claims to stand in the heritage of a Jeremiah or a Jesus must likewise "subvert" those structures around it that destroy the potential for personhood. It will be able to do so, if it does, only because it *has* "a place to stand," a deeper loyalty in the name of which it can challenge everything that contravenes the potential for personhood, whether racism, military budgets, corrupt courts, or politicians who debase the meaning of "national honor."

Arthur Gish, writing out of the Anabaptist tradition of Christian sectarianism, describes the stance with no holds barred:

> To be a Christian is to be a subversive, or at least that is how he will be viewed by society. Since his loyalty is to one who is beyond history, he cannot give his ultimate allegiance to any government, business, class, or any other institution. His views cannot be expected to coincide with the majority view around him. He can be expected to be in continual conflict with the structures of the society, for to be at peace with God means to be in conflict with the world. When a Christian is faithful to Christ and refuses compromise with the demands of society, it is almost inevitable that he will be looked upon by the power structures of that society as being disloyal and subversive, and so he is. He *is* a person who dares to call the whole society into question. He is a revolutionary (*The New Left and Christian Radicalism*, p. 113).

The God Who Takes Sides

Where can communities of creative dissent discover the resources to "subvert" in the name of a more fundamental loyalty? Clearly it will be because of the nature and quality of that fundamental loyalty. In the Jewish and Christian communities, the quality of the fundamental loyalty (and why it leads to subversion) is clear. Many words are used to describe the God of the Bible—he is a God of justice (so that injustice must be challenged), or a God of all the nations (so that nationalistic loyalties can never be ultimate), or a God of mercy (so that vindictiveness can never be man's final word). For our purposes, however, what is most characteristic of the God of the Bible is that he is *the God who takes sides.* He is not indifferent, he is not aloof, he is not uncaring. What happens to people matters to him. And if there is anything that is clear in the Biblical drama as a whole, it is that when God takes sides, he sides with the oppressed. Even his initial bias toward Israel is an example of this. God chooses Israel not because Israel is the greatest of the nations; Israel is in fact "the least of all the peoples," a tiny, insignificant nation, the doormat of the ancient world on which the great empires scuffed their boots. God chooses Israel simply because he loves Israel. We have already seen that when weak Israel was pitted against mighty Egypt, God did not side with the Pharaoh, the powerful political leader, but with the oppressed menial servants, the scum of society, the slaves.

So it goes in the New Testament as well. Mary sings the Magnificat, her song of praise to God, in the following terms:

> He has put down the mighty from their thrones, and exalted
> those of low degree; he has filled the hungry with good things,
> and the rich he has sent empty away (Luke 2:52-53).

When Jesus comes to Nazareth to preach, he takes the cue for his own mission from the prophet Isaiah, asserting that the Spirit of the Lord has annointed him "to preach good news to the *poor* . . . to proclaim release to the *captives*. . . to set at liberty those who are *oppressed*" (Luke 4:18). His own background is that of the *am ha'aretz*, the poor of the land. A favorite imagery to describe him is that of "servant." When he paints a picture of the Last Judgment and seeks to test the authenticity of the life of the nations, the criterion is not right belief or theological orthodoxy, but what has been done for the sick, the naked, the hungry, and the imprisoned.

The bias is clear beyond any doubt. God sides with the oppressed. The oppressors are on the wrong side. It is as clear as that. And as disturbing as that. For here is where the theological shoe begins to pinch: on how many contrasting lists of oppressors and oppressed are white middle-class Americans likely to be found in the second column rather than the first? Not many. So here is the point at which a significant identity crisis will continue to confront white middle-class Americans: do they find their true identity in terms of nation, race, and class, or in terms of the larger identity their religious community offers them?

Living in such a bind is never going to be easy, and perhaps the hardest thing of all is to clarify the meaning of membership in a community dedicated to the cause of the oppressed when the members themselves are not truly numbered among the oppressed. To face that problem means to face all sorts of disturbing new concerns. Is "identification with the oppressed" anything more than a guilt trip of middle-class romantics? Can any group really make decisions that threaten its own security, let alone its own continuation? Is there any way to avoid paternalism in reaching out to those in need? Can members of an affluent community really let go their affluence, or at least find ways to use it for the nonaffluent? How revolutionary are middle-class people really going to be?

Answers will be hard to come by, but unless the stance is pure hypocrisy, the questions had better continue to be asked.

Fomenters of Conflict or Agents of Reconciliation?

Many people suggest that the task of the religious community is to avoid conflict and to reconcile: it should not divide but unite; it should not create breaches between people but heal them; it should not be a center of agitation but a source of peace; it should not, in short, be a fomenter of conflict but an agent of reconciliation.

The concern is well taken, but the antithesis is false. Much that passes for reconciliation is phony reconciliation, covering up conflict by pretending it is not there rather than confronting it openly and honestly. In this view, genuine differences are superficially smoothed over as though they did not exist, with the result that the wound, rather than being healed (as may initially appear to be the case), festers more deeply than ever, and sooner or later is discovered to have spread so widely that it can no longer be contained.

Racial integration is a case in point. Integration in the early '60s was seen to be a reconciling reality, and superficially race relations appeared for a while to be greatly improved. But what the whites (who had the power and the numbers) had failed to see was that integration had been offered to the black *on the white man's terms*. Those blacks who conformed to white middle-class standards of language, dress, and hair style were welcomed into white middle-class society. Other blacks were not. Integration actually meant telling the black, "Cease to be who *you* are, act on the outside like a white person, and maybe whites will tolerate you in their neighborhoods, so long as you remain on your good behavior."

If that is a caricature, it is only a slight caricature. The point is that there was little *genuine* reconciliation going on in that kind of integration; the movement collapsed in the bitterness of blacks who thought they had been had and the hurt feelings of whites who thought they had been trying so hard. Genuine reconciliation between black and white will mean open acknowledgment of differences, recognition of genuine antagonisms, even a seeking out of those issues which divide rather than unite, since any reconciliation will be spurious that has not overcome genuine divisions rather than phony ones.

This is why the religious community can be the agent of reconciliation at the very moment that it appears to be a fomenter of conflict. It is not reconciliation to ignore structures of violence because calling attention to them might upset people and cause conflict. The conflict that the structural violence produces is far more critical than the disturbance to a few people in a church or synagogue. To be on the side of justice is going to make many people unhappy—particularly those who benefit from ongoing structures of injustice—and to be on the side of justice is thereby going to create conflict. But to ignore injustice in the name of avoiding *that kind* of conflict is merely to drive the injustice deeper into the social structures, and make more difficult the ultimate reconciliation. Thus the task of subversion, the task of engaging in deep-seated social challenge, is the only true route to genuine reconciliation, in which the true sources of conflict have been exposed and overcome.

Beyond Wisdom to Power

Thus far we have been talking about the religious community as the resource for a wider perspective, providing "a place to stand" and a series of new insights that might not otherwise be available. The religious community can be a source of *wisdom*.

But the religious community can also be a source of *power*. We have been using the word *power* in earlier chapters in a political sense to describe the means of bringing about change in society, and we have been insisting that such power has been too much the monopoly of a few small groups who have abused it for their own ends. In the present discussion, however, *power* is being used in the sense of the strength to take a stand, the willingness to risk oneself for an unpopular position, the courage to be open to fundamental change.

It is a familiar phenomenon in almost all religions that there is a gap between the "is" and the "ought." Paul states the dilemma classically when he informs his readers that he can will what is right but cannot do it: "I do not do what I want, but I do the very thing I hate. . . . I do not do the good I want, but the evil I do not want is what I do" (Romans 8:18-19). Wisdom, in other words, is not enough; it needs the complement of power. And this is something we do not seem to be able to supply for ourselves. Here is where religion, whether Judaism or Christianity, is never reducible simply to a matter of ethics, no matter how highly refined and sensitized. For the power is never just a matter of trying a little harder. It is always a gift. For the Jew, Jahweh continually offers himself to his people, judging sternly but also redeeming mercifully. For the Christian, empowerment comes through the gift of Christ, who cuts through the tangle of anxieties and mixed motives to create a new situation and a fresh start. In both cases it is a gift of "grace"—an unmerited new possibility that is not offered once and then withdrawn, but is continually offered and never withdrawn.

The elaboration of this theme would obviously take us far beyond the range of the present essay. What is important here is simply the recognition that within any mature religious perspective there is always the promise that power is available, and that this promise can keep us from despairing at the magnitude of the tasks that confront us. That individuals or groups will divest themselves of power (in the political sense of our earlier discussion) is one of the most unlikely prospects in human history. Few political scientists or politicians would count on it. And yet from a religious perspective there is always the fresh possibility that, in limited ways at least, such a breakthrough might occur as an unexpected fruit of "grace." If it is unlikely to characterize the life of a nation, it might occasionally characterize the life of the religious community. We hear the call of third-world theologians to their own churches to become "the Church of the poor." That is a stern demand to a Church that has lived an affluent existence for hundreds of years at the expense of most of the peasants. Even out of such unlikely antecedents, however, the call for such a turning is beginning to be heard. Perhaps it is not too late even for us.

Is There a Special Role for the White Churches?

We have insisted throughout that different groups in different situations can legitimately take different stands. The specific task of an American middle-class businessman who has a social conscience may be different from the task of a Colombian peasant who is being exploited by the businessman's company. Both may, for very different reasons, want the exploitation to stop. If so, they will clearly use different tactics in their different situations to achieve the mutually desired end.

The same thing will be true among the different groups who attack the problem of structural violence. It may be a Christian role to be willing to suffer, but it will be decidedly un-Christian to tell blacks that their present role is to suffer to bring about change; they have already done more than their share of suffering, and their concern must be to forge the tools of their own liberation. Whites cannot tell blacks how to do this any more than they can legislate attitudes for Chicanos or Brazilians. In the same way, Christians had better not be too ready to suggest costly stances for Jews, since Jews have also, particularly in terms of the holocaust of World War II, been victimized to an inordinate degree.

Thus it cannot be the task of a white middle-class Christian (which is what the author, for better or worse, is) to tell blacks or Chicanos or Brazilians or Jews just how they should deal with structural violence. But it can be the task, and indeed the obligation, of such an author to indicate what special tasks might be placed upon white middle-class churches. My own feeling, then, is that if white churches are going to do no more than reflect (in pale fashion) the values of the culture around them, they do not really deserve to survive; that they are going to have to look long and hard at where their real allegiances lie, and then make some basic choices in the near future. The choices, if properly made, will place the churches in jeopardy, for they will involve tremendous risks with no assurance of success.

To be as direct as possible, I see no less exacting task for white churches than that of seeking, at whatever cost, to embody *revolutionary nonviolent love*. Anything else is no longer worth the bother and can be done quite adequately by other groups in our society. If we are going to talk about a *special* role for the Church—a role that might make a difference to the human family—then nothing short of the stance of revolutionary nonviolent love will do.

(a) The stance must be *revolutionary*, for the middle-class structures to which most white churches belong clearly work against the well-being of a majority of the human family; if God is truly on the side of the oppressed, then most of his churches are presently working against those with whom he chooses to side, and are thus thwarting rather than furthering his will.

(b) The stance must be *nonviolent*. This is a conclusion based on both moral and pragmatic grounds: moral, since only as the last resort "when all else fails" is violence justified, and there are still opportunities for white churches to exert leverage short of violence on the structures of which they are a part; pragmatic, since at the present time in America a violent revolution (even if morally justified) would clearly be a disaster to those attempting it, as well as to the cause they represent. Bloodshed and defeat would be the only result.

(c) The stance must embody *love*, which is the operative word for the whole position. Love, as the gospel pictures it, is self-giving, offered without any assurance of reciprocation, identifying with the recipient, and even willing to risk the loss of all things for the sake of the recipient.

Such a description may seem completely out of touch with reality. How would it be fleshed out? Such a Church would acknowledge its complicity in the structures of violence around it, and would seek either to disengage from those structures or to change them, believing that the Holy Spirit can work through smoke-filled rooms in a political way the Biblical imagery never anticipated. It would attempt to see the world through the eyes of the oppressed, and would thus take its cues from a Helder Camara and a César Chávez rather than a Norman Vincent Peale or a Billy Graham. It would find ways to make its resources more fully available to the minorities it had helped to exploit, giving support to new black groups rather than putting new blacktop on its parish house parking lot. It would open its facilities to organizations serving the dispossessed in the community around it, rather than keeping such facilities locked up between Ladies' Aid teas. It would set itself against the Pentagon mentality of its nation's leaders, and actively repudiate, by civil disobedience if necessary, foreign policies that permitted a national leader to order the dropping of one thousand tons of bombs a day in the name of negotiating for peace. It might, in short, become increasingly unpopular in areas where it had previously courted popularity. But it might, even more shortly, regain its soul.

All of this is a tall order. It seems beyond the reach of all but the saintly, and it may seem naïve even to propose it. But it surely defines what the Church *ought* to be, and to settle for anything less as the norm will mean finally to justify whatever the Church now *is*—which in the fearful present is not enough.

At the same time, the vision may not be as naïve as first appears. For the stakes may be so high that W. H. Auden was merely describing the only alternatives available when he wrote, at the beginning of World War II, "We must love one another or die." In a world which rapidly escalates into unthinking and brutal violence at the drop of a bomb, there may be a crucial place for a community that will insist that *at whatever cost to itself* it will say "no" to violence, both the structural violence that silently devastates and the physical violence that shriekingly destroys. Such a position is going to be a minority position. It is not going to draw new members with noticeable rapidity, and if seriously embodied will drive out many who now feel they share the name of Christian. Those outside, or on the edges, of such a Church will feel threatened by it and may perhaps turn violently against it. At least they will no longer do what they presently do—ignore it.

To speak in this fashion is not a prelude to offering blueprints. It is not even to suggest that blueprints are available or could be drawn, given a little advance notice. For revolutionary nonviolent love is not reducible to blueprints or rules or instant specifications. But if it does not soon become an ingredient in the world of today, we can be sure there will be no world of tomorrow.

> *Did not your father eat and drink*
>   *and do justice and righteousness?*
> *Then it was well with him.*
> *He judged the cause of the poor and needy;*
>   *then it was well.*
> **Is this not to know me?**
>   *says the Lord.*

Yes.

ABOUT THE AUTHOR

A native of Carthage, Illinois, Robert McAfee Brown came to Stanford in 1962 after ten years on the faculty of Union Theological Seminary, where he received his divinity degree. He also holds an AB from Amherst and a PhD from Columbia University. A Presbyterian, he is the author of several books, including *The Spirit of Protestantism* and *The Ecumenical Revolution*, and he writes regularly for such journals as *The Commonweal, The Journal of Ecumenical Studies,* and *Christianity and Crisis*. His academic interests center on contemporary theology and its relation to other disciplines, Christian ethics, and Christian thought and contemporary theologians. Professor Brown believes in combat against apathy and his deepest concerns are the ecumenical movement and the struggle for social justice. He was an official Protestant observer at the second Vatican Council. He has recently resumed full-time teaching after serving as acting dean of the Stanford Chapel. Cited several times by members of the senior class as a favorite professor, he in 1966 was one of eight university professors across the nation to receive the Harbison Award of the Danforth Foundation, which "seeks to recognize and honor outstanding teacher-scholars who have been especially effective in demonstrating a concern for their students as individuals."

Reader's Guide

Because the literature on religion and violence is virtually endless, any "brief" biography must be arbitrary—a fact that can be justified only by the further fact that many of the books listed contain extensive bibliographies of their own. Those who disagree with the viewpoint of the present volume will find a wide variety of approaches and viewpoints in the books cited. There has been a conscious effort to avoid stacking the deck.

The topical headings are also arbitrary. Many of the books could be listed under several headings, as the descriptive comments make clear.

Overall Treatments of the Problem of Violence

Arendt, Hannah. *Crisis of the Republic*. New York: Harcourt Brace Jovanovich, 1972.
> A collection of penetrating essays on "Lying in Politics," "Civil Disobedience," "On Violence," and "Thoughts on Politics and Revolution"; all germane to the theme of violence and especially useful in demanding and exemplifying precision in the use of terms.

Bianchi, Eugene. *The Religious Experience of Revolutionaries*. Garden City, N.Y.: Doubleday, 1972.
> A creative integration of the experiences of Ché Guevara, Daniel Berrigan, Malcolm X, Martin Luther King, Abbie Hoffman, and Frantz Fanon, in which the issue of religion and violence is continually at the forefront of discussion.

Gray, Glenn. *On Understanding Violence Philosophically and Other Essays*. New York: Harper and Row, 1970.
> A brief but carefully reflective essay that delivers what its title promises.

Hartogs, Renatus, and Eric Artzt, eds. *Violence: Causes and Solutions*. New York: Dell, 1970.
> A psychologically oriented collection of essays dealing with "dimensions of violence" and ways of "understanding and controlling violence."

Hofstadter, Richard, and Michael Wallace, eds. *American Violence: A Documentary History*. New York: Random House, 1970.
> A full collection of first-hand reports of many violent episodes from

American history, including examples of political, economic, religious, racial, personal, and police violence.

May, Rollo. *Power and Innocence: A Search for the Source of Violence.* New York: Norton, 1972.
> A psychological study that provides important background for the issues discussed in the present book; particularly helpful on "the anatomy of violence."

National Commission on the Causes and Prevention of Violence. *To Establish Justice, To Ensure Domestic Tranquility.* Washington: U.S. Government Printing Office, 1969.
> Report of the Presidential Commission established in the wake of the murders of Martin Luther King and Robert Kennedy. Occasional recognition of the fact that injustice is the underlying cause of revolt and repression.

Rose, Thomas, ed. *Violence in America.* New York: Random House, 1971.
> A symposium with excellent essays on a theory and definition of violence, together with historical treatments of violence in American history, including the 1960s.

Shaffer, Jerome, ed. *Violence.* New York: David McKay, 1971.
> Four essays dealing with violence in a philosophical perspective with careful attention to definition of terms.

Sharp, Gene. *The Politics of Nonviolent Action.* Boston: Porter Sargent, 1973.
> A massive 1,000-page study of the power, methods, and dynamics of nonviolence as a social and political technique, prepared under the auspices of the Harvard University Center for International Affairs.

Sorel, Georges. *Reflections on Violence.* New York: Macmillan, 1961.
> An older (1908) socialist critique of existing society, written from a perspective that proposes violence as the only means to bring about the requisite social change.

Themes of War and Peace in Historical Perspective

Bainton, Roland. *Christian Attitudes to War and Peace.* Nashville: Abingdon, 1960.
> The most useful single treatment of the historical development of pacifism, the "just war," and the crusade. A standard reference.

Brandon, S. G. F. *Jesus and the Zealots.* New York: Scribner's, 1967.
> A strong case for aligning Jesus much more closely with the violent revolutionary Zealot movement than has usually been done. Controversial and thought-provoking. Useful in relation to the Cullmann and Edwards volumes cited below.

Cullmann, Oscar. *Jesus and the Revolutionaries.* New York: Harper and Row, 1970.
> A brief response to Brandon, affirming the revolutionary quality of Jesus' life and teaching, but denying the close relationship to the Zealots posited by Brandon.

Edwards, George. *Jesus and the Politics of Violence*. New York: Harper
and Row, 1972.
    A careful Biblical study, in large part a response to Brandon, suggesting
that Jesus was an apostle of nonviolent change and that his approach can
be adopted by 20th century Christians. Full bibliography.

Gray, Glenn. *The Warriors: Reflections on Men in Battle*. New York:
Harper and Row, 1970.
    A reflective and thoughtful account of what participation in war does to
men; by a philosopher who served as an intelligence officer in World
War II.

Long, Edward. *War and Conscience in America*. Philadelphia: Westminster Press, 1968.
    Brief and clear treatment of varying positions on war, indicating three
types of support and three types of opposition to participation in war.

Marrin, Albert, ed. *War and the Christian Conscience*. Chicago: Reg-
nery, 1971.
    A collection of primary sources "from Augustine to Martin Luther King,
Jr.," illustrating a variety of perspectives ranging from "The Christian
as Warrior" to "The Pacifist Tradition," with a section on new issues
posed in the atomic era.

MacGregor, G. H. C. *The New Testament Basis of Pacifism*. Nyack,
N.Y.: Fellowship of Reconciliation, 1954.
    A treatment of relevant Biblical passages, with the intent of showing that
pacifism is firmly grounded in Jesus' teaching and example.

Nuthall, Geoffrey. *Christian Pacifism in History*. Oxford: Blackwell,
1958.
    Brief historical survey of five varieties of Christian pacifism.

Potter, Ralph. *War and Moral Discourse*. Richmond: John Knox Press,
1969.
    A careful treatment of the ethics of warfare, with special attention to the
doctrine of the "just war" and problems of conscience. Has a full and
extraordinarily useful annotated bibliography that is an essential supple-
ment to the present one.

Shinn, Roger. *Wars and Rumors of Wars*. Nashville, Abingdon, 1972.
    An absorbing "war diary" from World War II, to which have been added
the author's reflections twenty-five years later as he deals afresh with
matters of conscience, violence, and war. An unusually thoughtful presentation.

Weber, Hans-Reudi. "Freedom Fighter or Prince of Peace?" *Study Encounter*, Vol. VIII, No. 4. Geneva: World Council of Churches, 1973.
    An extensive review article dealing with the themes raised in Brandon,
Cullmann, and Edwards.

Yoder, John. *The Politics of Jesus*. Grand Rapids: Eerdmans, 1972.
    A careful and well-documented treatment of Jesus' teachings, written
from a pacifist perspective.

Contemporary Theological Approaches to Violence and Nonviolence

Albrecht, Paul, and M. M. Thomas, eds. *World Conference on Church and Society (Christians in the Technical and Social Revolutions of Our Time).* Geneva: World Council of Churches, 1967.

Official report of the "Geneva Conference" that opened up the issue of Christian involvement in violent revolution. A seminal source for all subsequent discussion.

Barkat, Anwar, ed. *Conflict, Violence and Peace.* Geneva: World Council of Churches, 1970.

Papers given at an ecumenical consultation on "Alternatives to Violence in the Quest for Peace" by representatives from all parts of the world.

Berger, Peter, and Richard Neuhaus. *Movement and Revolution.* New York: Doubleday, 1970.

Essays from "conservative" and "radical" standpoints about the transformation of society. Neuhaus' essay applies seven criteria of traditional "just war theory" to the problem of participation by violent means in a contemporary "just revolution."

Cone, James. *Black Theology and Black Power.* New York: Seabury Press, 1970.

An impassioned plea for a distinctive "black theology" that is important, if disturbing, reading for whites, with continual reflection upon the problem of violence in achieving liberation from oppression.

Douglass, James. *The Non-Violent Cross.* New York: Macmillan, 1968.

A collection of essays making a strong case for pacifism as the authentic Christian position and attacking such halfway houses as the "just war."

Ellul, Jacques. *Violence.* New York: Seabury Press, 1969.

A strong attack on recent attempts to provide a theological rationale for Christian participation in revolutionary violence. Sharply critical of the Geneva conference report cited above. (See also the response by M. M. Thomas in *The Ecumenical Review*, April 1971, pp. 188-90.)

Gish, Arthur. *The New Left and Christian Radicalism.* Grand Rapids: Eerdmans, 1970.

A historical and contemporary analysis of radicalism, attempting to synthesize "new left" and Anabaptist thought. Contains a consideration of relevant Biblical resources, and makes the case for "a revolution of nonviolence."

IDOC. *When All Else Fails: Christian Arguments on Violent Revolution.* Philadelphia: Pilgrim Press, 1970.

A variety of essays and documents, including a number from Latin America, expounding and analyzing a range of positions on social protest. A very useful collection.

King, Martin Luther. *Stride Toward Freedom.* New York: Harper and Row, 1958.

The chapter on "Pilgrimage to Nonviolence" is particularly important as an account of the development of King's own position.

Marty, Martin, and Dean Peerman, eds. *New Theology No. 6.* New York: Macmillan, 1969.

A collection of essays from varying perspectives dealing with war, revolution, violence, pacifism, etc. A useful introduction to many of the problems.

Merton, Thomas. *Faith and Violence*. Notre Dame, Ind.: University of Notre Dame Press, 1968.

> Essays on "a theology of resistance," Vietnam, "from nonviolence to black power," and "violence and the death of God," by a Roman Catholic monk who became a strong proponent of nonviolence.

Miller, W. R. *Nonviolence: A Christian Interpretation*. New York: Schocken, 1966.

> The fullest single treatment of nonviolence, with a great number of case studies on the specific application of nonviolent methods to producing social change. Has a useful bibliography.

Moltmann, Jürgen. *Religion, Revolution and the Future*. New York: Scribner's, 1969.

> The essay on "God and Revolution" is particularly helpful on the theme of violence.

Ramsay, Paul. *War and the Christian Conscience*. Durham: Duke University Press, 1961.

> An early attempt to rehabilitate the "just war" theory for contemporary use.

———. *The Just War: Force and Political Responsibility*. New York: Scribner's, 1968.

> A recent collection of essays that generally defend Christian participation in war, including the war in Vietnam.

Rasmussen, Larry. *Dietrich Bonhoeffer: Reality and Resistance*. Nashville: Abingdon, 1972.

> A well-documented and critical account of Bonhoeffer's shift from pacifism to a willingness to participate in the plot against Hitler's life.

Régamey, P. *Non-Violence and the Christian Conscience*. New York: Herder and Herder, 1966.

> A reflective blending of a Gandhian approach and a Christian context.

SODEPAX. *Peace: The Desperate Imperative*. Geneva: Committee on Society, Development and Peace, 1969.

> Report of a consultation on "Christian Concern for Peace" held in Baden, Austria, in 1970; a good summary of recent ecumenical thinking.

Swomley, John. *Liberation Ethics*. New York: Macmillan, 1972.

> An examination of the role of violence in producing revolutionary change, written from a solidly informed pacifist perspective and stressing the need for structural change throughout society.

Civil Disobedience

Berrigan, Daniel. *The Trial of the Catonsville Nine*. Boston: Beacon Press, 1970.

> A condensation of the court transcript of one of the classic recent instances of civil disobedience in the name of moral concern. The testimony of the nine defendants illustrates the reasons for increasing radicalization in seeking to effect social change.

Dellinger, Dave. *Revolutionary Nonviolence*. New York: Doubleday, 1971.

Essays spanning a quarter of a century by one of the most articulate practitioners of nonviolence and civil disobedience. Material drawn from the author's experience in relation to World War II, Vietnam, Cuba, China, and the Chicago Democratic Convention in 1968.

Gray, Francine du Plessix. *Divine Disobedience.* New York: Random House, 1971.

An absorbing study of individuals and movements on the "Catholic left" with special attention to Philip and Daniel Berrigan.

Hall, Robert. *The Morality of Civil Disobedience.* New York: Harper and Row, 1971.

A careful study of civil disobedience, taking seriously the place of law in society and yet recognizing that when law is the instrument of privilege rather than justice there can be a moral obligation to challenge it.

Stevick, Daniel. *Civil Disobedience and the Christian.* New York: Seabury, 1969.

An attempt "to argue that there are some situations in which civil disobedience is an allowable consideration or an actual duty, to plead for understanding and support for those who are convinced that they are in one of those situations now, to provide criteria by which a person might be assisted in determining that he was or was not obliged to engage in a conscientious violation of law, and to suggest considerations which might make such an action more, rather than less, responsible." Full notes and an annotated bibliography.

Thoreau, Henry. *Civil Disobedience.* Many editions.

Tolstoy, Leo. *Tolstoy's Writings on Civil Disobedience and Nonviolence.* New York: New American Library, 1968.

Two of the "classic" treatments of the problem, from which most contemporary discussions start.

Issues of Development and Economic Aid

Bauer, Gerhard, ed. *Towards a Theology of Development.* Geneva: Committee on Society, Development and Peace, 1970.

An exhaustive bibliography of over 2,000 items, topically arranged. An indispensable tool to further study of the problems of theology and development.

Bryant, M. Darrol. *A World Broken by Unshared Bread.* Geneva: World Council of Churches, 1970.

Helpful compilation of theology, political-economic analysis, and useful but disturbing statistics.

Dickinson, Richard. *Line and Plummet: The Churches and Development.* Geneva: World Council of Churches, 1968.

Overall survey of the issues, prepared for the Uppsala Assembly in 1968.

Gollwitzer, Helmut. *The Rich Christians and Poor Lazarus.* New York: Macmillan, 1970.

Creative and critical comments on the Uppsala Assembly of the World Council of Churches and its treatment of the themes of revolution, politics, poverty, and economic aid.

Gruber, Pamela, ed. *Fetters of Injustice.* Geneva: World Council of Churches, 1970.

> Report of a consultation on ecumenical assistance to development projects, with individual papers and working group reports.

IDOC International (North American Edition), 239 E. 49th Street, New York, 10017.

> A biweekly collection of documents from all parts of the world dealing with "human and religious renewal" and covering such topics as violence, economic aid, racism, and third-world liberation. An essential tool for keeping abreast of contemporary thinking.

Laurentin, René. *Liberation, Development and Salvation.* Maryknoll, N.Y.: Orbis Books, 1972.

> A full treatment of theological issues raised by the need for economic aid, with a separate chapter on violence. The preface provides an important updating of the original text.

Munby, Denys, ed. *World Development: Challenge to the Churches.* Washington: Corpus Books, 1969.

> Papers prepared for the Beirut Conference on Society, Development and Peace (SODEPAX) together with the official report of the conference.

Preston, Ronald, ed. *Technology and Social Justice.* Valley Forge: Judson Press, 1971.

> A large collection of essays on the social and economic teaching of the Geneva and Uppsala conferences of the World Council of Churches, with extensive sections on development and economic aid.

SODEPAX. *In Search of a Theology of Development.* Geneva: Commission on Society, Development and Peace, 1969.

> Critical papers and reports presented at an ecumenical consultation.

SODEPAX. *Partnership or Privilege? An Ecumenical Reaction to the Second Development Decade.* Geneva: Commission on Society, Development and Peace, 1970.

> An intensive survey and critique of an initial decade of development with an eye to avoiding similar mistakes during the second decade.

Van Leeuwen, Arend. *Development Through Revolution.* New York: Scribner's, 1970.

> An exceedingly useful treatment of themes growing out of the Geneva Conference with special attention to development, revolution, and war, showing some of the pitfalls of trying to resolve the issues through economic aid.

"Third World" Literature That Contributes to an Understanding of the Problem of Violence

Alves, Reubem. *A Theology of Human Hope.* Washington: Corpus Books, 1969.

> The first substantial "third world" theological contribution to be made available in English; takes European-Anglo-Saxon theological perspectives and translates them into a theology for human freedom seen in the realities of political and social oppression.

Camara, Helder. *Church and Colonialism*. London: Sheed and Ward, 1969.

A collection of essays by the outstanding proponent of revolutionary non-violence in Latin America; see especially Chapter 10, "Violence—the Only Way?"

———. *Spiral of Violence*. Denville, N.J.: Dimension Books, 1971.

A brief treatment of the theme of violence growing out of an analysis of the "third world" situation. Develops the three-fold distinction between injustice, revolt, and repression discussed in the present volume.

Fanon, Frantz. *The Wretched of the Earth*. New York: Grove Press, 1968.

An impassioned defense of violence as a means by which the dispossessed can regain their human dignity, though the author qualifies his thesis more significantly than most reports on the book acknowledge.

Freire, Paulo. *Pedagogy of the Oppressed*. New York: Herder and Herder, 1972.

A difficult but intensely rewarding book about using education for the liberation rather than the ongoing oppression of Latin American peasants. Has important but uncomfortable implications for education elsewhere.

Gerassi, John, ed. *Revolutionary Priest: The Complete Writings and Messages of Camilo Torres*. New York: Random House, 1971.

A chronological compilation tracing the radicalization of a Roman Catholic priest from a comfortable middle-class upbringing to becoming a member of the armed guerrilla forces, with whom he was shot and killed. Includes an interpretive introduction by the editor.

Gutiérrez, Gustavo. *A Theology of Liberation*. Maryknoll, N.Y.: Orbis Books, 1972.

A large and extraordinarily helpful treatment of the theme, containing not only political-sociological analysis but a full theological rationale for the movement from "development" to "liberation." The most important work in its field.

Hageman, Alice, and Philip Wheaton, eds. *Religion in Cuba Today*. New York: Association Press, 1971.

Essays by Cubans on the role of the church before, during, and after a contemporary revolution.

Houtart, François, and André Rousseau. *The Church and Revolution*. Maryknoll, N.Y.: Orbis Books, 1971.

An overall treatment of the theme, with illustrative material on various revolutionary episodes including "The Cuban Revolution" and "The Revolutionary Movements in Latin America," by Roman Catholic sociologists.

Morris, Colin. *Unyoung, Uncolored, Unpoor*. Nashville: Abingdon, 1970.

A vigorous presentation of the case for violence as a means of gaining liberation, written by a British missionary to Zambia out of his first-hand observation of white exploitation of blacks.

MacEoin, Gary. *Revolution Next Door: Latin America in the 1970's*. New York: Holt, Rinehart and Winston, 1971.

A report on the entire continent by a knowledgeable Roman Catholic journalist, with special attention to the role of the Church. Helpful annotated bibliography.

Peruvian Bishops' Commission for Social Action. *Between Honesty and Hope.* Maryknoll, N.Y.: Maryknoll, 1970.
The most useful single collection of primary source materials from Latin America, with essays by groups and individuals, along with many texts from the crucial Medellín Conference of the Latin American Episcopate in 1968.

Other Works Cited

Bennett, John. "Siding with the Oppressors," *Christianity and Crisis,* Vol. 32, No. 5, April 3, 1972.

Berrigan, Daniel. *America Is Hard to Find.* Garden City, N.Y.: Doubleday, 1972.

———. *Night Flight to Hanoi.* New York: Macmillan, 1968.

British Council of Churches. *Violence in South Africa: A Christian Assessment.* London: SCM Press, 1970.

Brown, D. Mackenzie. *Ultimate Concern: Tillich in Dialogue.* New York: Harper and Row, 1965.

Brown, Robert McAfee. *Frontiers for the Church Today.* New York: Oxford University Press, 1973.

———. *The Pseudonyms of God.* Philadelphia: Westminster Press, 1972.

Gutiérrez, Gustavo. "Notes for a Theology of Liberation," *Theology Digest,* Vol. 19, No. 2 (Summer 1971).

Miguez-Bonino, José. *The Development Apocalypse. Risk,* Vol. III, No. 1-2. Geneva: World Council of Churches, 1967.

Mounier, Emmanual. *L'Engagement de la Foi,* Vol. 1. Paris: Seuil, 1933.

Tillich, Paul. *Dynamics of Faith.* New York: Harper and Row, 1957.

———. *Systematic Theology,* Vol. 1. Chicago: University of Chicago Press, 1957.

World Council of Churches. "Violence, Nonviolence and the Struggle for Social Justice," *Study Encounter,* Vol. 7, No. 3, 1971.